D0934760

LEGENDS OF NEW ENGLAND

LEGENDS OF NEW ENGLAND

(1831)

BY

JOHN GREENLEAF WHITTIER

A FACSIMILE REPRODUCTION

WITH AN INTRODUCTION

BY

JOHN B. PICKARD

GAINESVILLE, FLORIDA

SCHOLARS' FACSIMILES & REPRINTS

1965

SCHOLARS' FACSIMILES & REPRINTS

1605 N.W. 14TH AVENUE

GAINESVILLE, FLORIDA, U.S.A.

HARRY R. WARFEL, GENERAL EDITOR

L.C. CATALOG CARD NUMBER: 65-12302

MANUFACTURED IN THE U.S.A.

TYPESETTING BY J. N. ANZEL, INC.

LITHOPRINTING BY EDWARDS BROTHERS

BINDING BY UNIVERSAL-DIXIE BINDERY

INTRODUCTION

In later life when Whittier reread his first published book, *Legends of New England*, he dryly re-
marked that it "seemed like somebody else" and on
another occasion spent five dollars for a copy in
order to burn it. Certainly his mature dismissal
of the book, his refusal to allow reprinting, and
modern critical disparagement of its artistic merit
seem mainly justified. However, as one pioneer
attempt to quarry in the rich field of New England
legend and as a culmination of Whittier's appren-
ticeship writing, the book demands reprinting and
restudy.

When the *Legends of New England* appeared in
February, 1831, Whittier had been publishing poetry
and prose for nearly five years. In this period he
had matured from a shy, uneducated Quaker farm-
boy to the highly respected editor of one of New
England's leading newspapers, who moved freely
within Hartford's cosmopolitan literary circles. Inspired by the current vogue for romantic writers
and somewhat inflated by the popular response to
his newspaper verses, Whittier printed over two
hundred poems in these years. Earlier, while re-

v

siding in Haverhill, he had planned an edition of his poetry and undoubtedly still hoped that poetic fame lay ahead. Characteristically, his aspirations exceeded his meagre technical ability and vacillating poetic interests. His conventional lyrics on poetic fancy and unrequited love, his Byronic posturizing, and sentimental imitations of Mrs. Sigourney's poetry illustrate their unsuitability to his poetic temperament. Yet in his first book he instinctively treated the New England material that ultimately proved most congenial to his poetic bent.

The book attempts to capture the romance and inherent poetic quality hidden within familiar oral traditions, local legends, Essex County superstitions, and historic incidents. Here Whittier struck the rich vein of folk material that was to be the substance for his best ballads and domestic poems like "Skipper Ireson's Ride" and "Telling the Bees." As the preface states, he compiled these tales to preserve selected examples of native lore, then fast disappearing, and to encourage other writers in making similar collections. Actually, he hoped for much more than this modest preface revealed. Certainly he desired to artistically limn the folk culture of northern New England as John G. C. Brainard had recently done for Connecticut traditions and to emulate the success of Washington Irving's collections of native legends. Like so many apologists for an embryonic American literature, Whittier claimed that his country's past contained the materials of romantic poetry and much more. He prophetically wrote in the ending of "The Mother's Revenge": "And the time is coming, when all these traditions shall be treasured up as a sacred legacy—when the tale of the Indian inroad and perils of the hunter—of the sublime courage and dark superstitions of our ancestors, will be listened to with an interest unknown to the present generation" (p. 130). *Legends of New England* is Whittier's ambitious attempt to demonstrate the poetic validity of local material.

Proper subject matter and an earnest conviction do not insure inspired writing or competent artistry. Most of the tales in the book are marred by Whittier's crude technical execution, digressive structure, and moralizing tone. The range of themes indicates his susceptibility to Gothic situations and sentimental romance: specter ships, doomed lovers, Indian atrocities, possessed animals, frontier massacres, demonic assemblies, and haunted houses. Of the eighteen pieces in the collection seven were prose sketches, while the remaining eleven were poems. Some effort was made to alternate a prose sketch with a poem and to group the tales thematically, but this hardly gave a definite pattern or thematic structure to the whole. The prose pieces are, undeniably, the weakest legends in the book. Here Whittier's fondness for digression, his inability to develop character, and the slighting of meaningful detail for sensational incident are most glaringly displayed. Four of the sketches deal with historical incidents or legends about Indian warfare and black magic, while the other three handle witch and animal superstitions. In one of the more interesting of these tales, "The Rattlesnake Hunter," Whittier treats an ancient folk tale of the rattlesnake's ability to charm its victims. The story is narrated by an old hunter who explains his passionate hatred for rattlesnakes. In almost Hawthornesque fashion it opens with a description of the hunter's snakelike physical characteristics. The climax where the hunter first succumbs to the fascination of the snake's rhythm, thereby causing the death of his young wife, is presented by most effective color and music imagery. The physical action is not sufficiently linked with the moral implications, nor is the influence of evil and the supernatural probed as in Hawthorne's "Egotism; or, the Bosom Serpent." Another prose sketch, "The Haunted House," though marred by a sentimental love plot, illustrates Whittier's fascination with witch superstitions. His concluding exposure of human credulity foreshadows his mature treatment of the witchcraft delusion in *Margaret Smith's Journal*. One other sketch, dealing with the winter attack of starving wolves, anticipates Willa Cather's insert about Pavel and Peter's harrowing experience in *My Antonia*. The loose form of the sketches allowed Whittier opportunity to digress on the value of superstitions and to record his sense of achievement in preserving a vanishing tradition. For many of the tales Whittier appended notes indicating his sources and explaining allusions as any good folklorist would do.

Although the eleven poems handle similar themes, they are far superior to the prose sketches in selection of detail, organization, and organic development of image and metaphor. There is even some slight experimentation with stanzaic and verse forms, as variations from the usual ballad pattern. The two poems treating apparitions, "The Murdered Lady" and "The Unquiet Sleeper," are the weakest of the group. Here Whittier depended upon bathos and sentimentality to depict the murder of a captive gentlewoman by pirates and the mysterious death of a hunter. Nor are his four Indian poems much better. "Metacom" is a typical example of Whittier's faltering attempts to dress his Indians in "Sir Walter Scott's plaid." The narrative relates Metacom's stoic endurance of a crushing defeat and his prophetic curse upon the white victors. However, the declamatory manner of presentation and continual reliance upon literary diction and shopworn images make Metacom a melodramatic poseur rather than a noble, somewhat tragic, warrior. Sentimentality and rhapsodic language also weaken the other poems concerned with the *ubi sunt* theme of lost Indian greatness. For example, "The Indian's Tale," told by the last survivor, is an undistinguished account of a plague which depleted a New England tribe. Yet beyond the artificiality and rhetoric in this poem (and also in "The Last Norridgewock" and "The White Mountains") there are moments of simple narration and dramatic emphasis that engender a pathos for the vanquished Indians.

Potentially one of the best poems in the book and in an entirely different vein is "The Weird Gathering." Here the basic situation bears an amazing resemblance to the superstition that Hawthorne immortalized in "Young Goodman Brown," an assembly of demons held to admit new members. Whittier carefully describes the grim wilderness of the meeting place as Satan trumpets his followers to the spot. Like Goodman Brown a young outsider dazedly watches the frightful assembly of wizards, gypsies, Indians, and demons, as dimly viewed under a baleful red glare. The stranger's unexplained presence where neither pagans nor Christians dare venture parallels Brown's inexplicable wandering out on Halloween. As he watches, a young girl seals her compact with Satan and is received into the witches' communion with "one dark spot of blood-red hue/Burned on her forehead fair." Her one demand is for vengeance on the man who has presumably seduced her. Conveniently the unknown observer proves to be her betrayer. Her revenge is a subtle one, for the seducer is to remain alive, eternally tormented by the memory of her doomed soul and without any capacity for human love. The curse takes immediate effect.

The anticlimatic conclusion bypasses the complex moral ambiguity that raises "Young Goodman Brown" to such effective artistic heights. Instead, Whittier merely catalogues the man's repentant death, while the girl is hanged as a witch. Characteristically Whittier adds a footnote that the gallows-tree was "blasted and dead with years—the heart of the wood only visible, like a gaunt skeleton, blackened by exposure to sun and storm," which is precisely the kind of physical detail that Hawthorne would have highlighted in the tale itself. Flawed as the poem is by conventional diction, it demonstrates Whittier's groping efforts to uncover the artistic gold hidden in the crude ore of folk narrative. A poetic failure, indeed, but one which deserves to be included in Whittier's collected works and read by all students of American poetry.

Two other poems dealing with specter ships and phantom warriors invite examination, since a mature Whittier was to rework these same subjects into good ballads. Some idea of Whittier's poetic growth is given by comparing "The Spectre Warriors" with "The Garrison of Cape Ann" (1857) or "The Spectre Ship" with "The Palatine" (1867) and "The Dead Ship of Harpswell" (1866). The earlier poem on the specter warriors concentrates on the dramatic appearance of phantom savages, but Whittier's sentimental characterization of the Puritan soldiers, his generalized descriptions, and his trite diction minimize the suspense and terror inherent in the legend. Also, the concluding four stanzas blunt the climax with their moralizations about the power of evil and the efficacy of prayer. By contrast a mature Whittier utilizing the same situation in "The Garrison of Cape Ann" graphically depicts the Massachusetts coast line with its "gleaming sand-drift, jagged capes, with bush and tree,/Leaning inland from the smiting of the wild and gusty sea." Instead of a vague fortress the garrison has a gabled roof and is made of unhewn timbers. The Puritan heroes and shrinking maids are replaced by real soldiers who eat "venison haunch" and drink from pewter tankards. To hasten the long night the men relate ghost tales, always returning to the strange Indian apparitions who have been attacking the fort. When another assault comes, the Captain in the best folk tradition shoots the fabled "silver button" to dispel the evil spirits. Only when that fails and another fusillade has no effect, do the Puritan soldiers request divine help. Even Whittier's habitual "moral squint" seems more a philosophic musing about the "dual life of old" than a didactic finish. Here the mature writer realized the artistic potential of the material as the aspiring poet never could.

The best poem of the collection is "The Black Fox." In this tale the rhetorical flourishes, literary allusions, and stereotyped images are replaced with a bare, simple diction and directness of narration that truly displays Whittier's ballad capacities. For

once Whittier carefully controls his narrative, estab-
lishing a realistic framework for the tale. A rural
family is seen assembled around a fire on a cold
winter's night, while the young children beg their
"Grandame" for a tale of the supernatural. With
the sparse language and simple wonder of an old
country woman, she relates the legend of the black
fox and his evil powers. The narrative moves quickly from the first appearance of the fox who mysteriously eludes the marksman's bullets to the Indian's
prophecies about the fox's magic powers. The
grandmother then describes the confident departure
of two young hunters who set out in a blinding snow-
storm to capture the fox. They fail to return and
in the spring a ragged wanderer, pursued by some
hidden terror, comes to her home, only to leave suddenly after mentioning the black fox. His appearance foreshadows the discovery of the two frozen
hunters and their subsequent burial in a place forever haunted by the diabolic fox. The tale closes
effectively with a final image of the fox howling
vindictively over the grave. Also woven within the
poem are some telling imagistic contrasts: the fox's
frightening blackness chills the warm red cheer of
the family fire, while the open confidence of the two
young hunters is dispelled by the deceptive white
purity of the snow which brings isolation and death.
Finally the arrival of spring is blighted by the presence of the crazed wanderer whose madness illumi-
nates the pervasive power of evil in the world. In

this poem, at least, Whittier had found his true métier, creating "Flemish pictures of old days" out of local superstitions and simple domestic affections. Perhaps if the book had received some popular acclaim or been extensively reviewed Whittier might have been encouraged to pursue these topics earlier than he did. The one known review in the *New York Mirror* (March 19, 1831) called the book one of the "most agreeable works of the kind we have read since the days of the Sketch Book," but censured Whittier for his lack of authentic research. As it was, nearly twenty years of abolitionist work and propaganda verses were to interpose before he would return to the "lays of my home."

In general this collection of sketches and poems foreshadows the future balladist that Whittier was to become. Also the book deserves attention as one of the pioneer efforts to preserve specimens of New England folklore and legend. Perhaps the best way to view the book is not to measure its achievement against his later work or to contrast it with Hawthorne's superior handling of similar material, but to highlight what Whittier achieved. The book attests the validity of Whittier's belief that local traditions merited preservation and contained the substance of good poetry and romance.

JOHN B. PICKARD

University of Florida
August, 1964

LEGENDS OF NEW ENGLAND

(1831)

BY

JOHN GREENLEAF WHITTIER

LEGENDS

OF

NEW-ENGLAND.

———— " The aged crone
Mixing the true and doubtful into one,
Tells how the Indian scalped the helpless child
And bore its shrieking mother to the wild,
How drums and flags and troops were seen on high
Wheeling and charging in the northern sky.—
How by the thunder-blasted tree was hid
The golden spoils of far famed Robert Kid;
And then the chubby grand-child wants to know
About the ghosts and witches long ago."

BRAINARD.

BY JOHN G. WHITTIER.

𝔥𝔞𝔯𝔱𝔣𝔬𝔯𝔡.

PUBLISHED BY HANMER AND PHELPS.

Sold by Packard & Butler, Hartford ; Carter, Hendee & Babcock, Boston ;
G. & C. & H. Carvill, and E. Bliss, New-York ; E. L. Carey, and
A Hart, Philadelphia ; and by the Booksellers generally.

1831.

PREFACE.

In the following pages I have attempted to present in an interesting form some of the popular traditions and legends of New-England. The field is a new one—and I have but partially explored it. New-England is rich in traditionary lore—a thousand associations of superstition and manly daring and romantic adventure, are connected with her green hills and her pleasant rivers. I leave the task of rescuing these associations from oblivion to some more fortunate individual; and if this little volume shall have the effect to induce such an effort, I shall at least be satisfied, whatever may be the judgment of the public upon my own humble production.

I have in many instances alluded to the superstition and bigotry of our ancestors— the rare and bold race who laid the foundation of this republic; but no one can accuse me of having done injustice to their memories. A son of New-England, and

proud of my birth-place, I would not wil-
lingly cast dishonor upon its founders.—
My feelings in this respect, have already
been expressed, in language, which 1 shall
be pardoned I trust for introducing in this
place :

Oh—never may a son of thine,
Where'e his wandering steps incline,
Forget the sky which bent above
His childhood like a dream of love—
The stream beneath the green hill flowing—
The broad-armed trees above it growing—
The clear breeze through the foliage blowing :—
Or, hear unmoved the taunt of scorn,
Breathed o'er the brave New-England born ;
Or mark the stranger's Jaguar hand
　Disturb the ashes of thy dead—
The buried glory of a land
　Whose soil with noble blood is red,
　And sanctified in every part,
Nor feel resentment, like a brand,
　Unsheathing from his fiery heart !

An apology is even in worse taste than a
preface ; but I would simply state that this
volume was written during the anxieties
and perplexing cares attendant upon the
management of a political and literary pe-
riodical.

CONTENTS.

LEGENDS

OF

NEW-ENGLAND.

THE MIDNIGHT ATTACK.

"Shrieks—fiendish yells!—they stab them in their sleep!"—DANA.

ONE hundred years ago!—How has New-England changed with the passing by of a single century! At first view, it would seem like the mysterious transform- ations of a dream, or like the strange mutations of sunset-clouds upon the face of the Summer Heavens. One hundred years ago!—The Oak struck its roots deeply in the Earth, and tossed its branches loftily in the sunshine, where now the voice of industry and enterprise rises in one perpetual murmur. The shad- ows of the forest lay brown and heavily, where now the village church-spire overtops the dwellings cluster- ed about it. Instead of the poor, dependent and fee- ble colonists of Britain, we are now a nation of our- selves—a people, great and prosperous and happy.

And those who battled with our fathers, or smoked the pipe of peace in their dwellings, where are they? Where is the mighty people which, but a little time ago, held dominion over this fair land, from the great lakes to the Ocean? Go to the hunting grounds of Miantonimoh and Annawon—to the royal-homes of Massasoit and Metacom and Sassacus, and ask for the traces and the memorials of the iron race of warriors, who wrestled with the pale Yengeese even unto death. There will perhaps remain the ruin of their ancient forts--the fragments of their ragged pottery—the stone-heads of their scattered arrows; and, here and there, on their old battle-fields, the white bones of their slain! And these will be all—all that remain to tell of the perished race of hunters and warriors. The Red Man has departed forever. The last gleam of his Council-fire has gone up from amidst the great oaks of the forest, and the last ripple of his canoe vanished from the pleasant waters bosomed among them. His children are hastening towards the setting of the Sun; and the plough-share of the stranger is busy among the bones of his fathers.

One hundred years ago!--The hunter, who ranged the hills and the forests of New-England, fought against other enemies, than the brown bear and the panther. The husbandman, as he toiled in the plain.

or the narrow clearing, kept closely at his side a loaded weapon; and wrought diligently and firmly in the midst of peril. The frequent crack of the Indian's rifle was heard in the still depths of the forest—the death-knell of the unwary hunter; and, ever and anon, the flame of some devoted farm-house, whose dwellers had been slaughtered by a merciless foe, rose redly upon the darkness of the night-time. The wild, and fierce eyes of the heathen gleamed through the thick underwood of the forest, upon the passing by of the worshippers of the only true God; and the war-whoop rang shrill and loud under the very walls of the sanctuary of prayer.

Perhaps no part of New-England affords a wider field for the researches of the Legendary, than that portion of Massachusetts Bay, formerly known as the province of Maine. There, the ferocious Norridge-wock held his stern councils, and there the tribes of the Penobscot went forth with song and dance to do battle upon the white man. There, the romantic and chivalrous Castine immured himself in the forest soli-tudes, and there the high-hearted Ralle—the mild and gifted Jesuit—gathered together the broken strength of the Norridgewock, and built up in the great wil-derness a temple to the true God. There too, he per-ished in the dark onslaught of the Colonists—perished with many wounds, at the very foot of the Cross, which his own hands had planted. And there, the Norridgewocks fell—one after another—in stern and uncomplaining pride—neither asking, nor giving quarter, as they resisted the white spoiler upon the threshold of their consecrated place of worship; and in view of their wives and their children.

The following is one among many legends of the strange rencounters of the White Man and the Indian, which are yet preserved in the ancient records and traditions of Maine. The simple and unvarnished narrative is only given.

It was a sultry evening towards the last of June, 172-, that Capt. Harmon and his Eastern rangers, urged their canoes up the Kennebeck River, in pursuit of their savage enemies. For hours they toiled diligently at the oar.—The last trace of civilization was left behind, and the long shadows of the skirting forests met and blended in the middle of the broad stream, which wound darkly through them. At every sound from the adjacent shores—the rustling wing of some night-bird, or the quick footsteps of some wild beast—the dash of the oar was suspended, and the ranger's grasp tightened on his rifle. All knew the peril of the enterprise; and that silence, which is natural to men, who feel themselves in the extreme of mortal jeopardy, settled like a cloud upon the midnight adventurers.

"Hush—softly men!" said the watchful Harmon, in a voice, which scarcely rose above a hoarse whisper, as his canoe swept round a ragged promontory, "there is a light ahead!"

All eyes were bent towards the shore. A tall Indian fire gleamed up amidst the great oaks, casting a red and strong light upon the dark waters. For a single and breathless moment the operation of the oar was suspended; and every ear listened with painful earnestness to catch the well known sounds, which seldom failed to indicate the propinquity of the savages. But all was now silent. With slow and faint movements of the oar, the canoes gradually approached the suspected spot. The landing was effected in silence. After moving cautiously for a considerable distance in the dark shadow, the party at length ventured within the broad circle of the light, which at first attracted their attention. Harmon was at their head, with an eye and a hand, quick as those of the savage enemy whom he sought.

The body of a fallen tree lay across the path. As the rangers were on the point of leaping over it, the hoarse whisper of Harmon again broke the silence.

"God of Heaven!" he exclaimed, pointing to the

2*

tree—"See here!—'tis the work of the cursed red skins!"

A smothered curse growled on the lips of the rangers, as they bent grimly forward in the direction pointed out by their commander. Blood was sprinkled on the rank grass, and a human hand—the hand of a white man,—lay on the bloody log!

There was not a word spoken, but every countenance worked with terrible emotion. Had the rangers followed their own desperate inclination, they would have hurried recklessly onward to the work of vengeance; but the example of their leader, who had regained his usual calmness and self-command, prepared them for a less speedy, but more certain triumph. Cautiously passing over the fearful obstacle in the pathway, and closely followed by his companions, he advanced stealthily and cautiously upon the light, hiding himself and his party as much as possible behind the thick trees. In a few moments they obtained a full view of the object of their search. Stretched at their length, around a huge fire, but at a convenient distance from it, lay the painted and half naked forms of twenty savages. It was evident from their appearance, that they had passed the day in one of their horrid revels; and that they were now suffering under the effects of intoxication. Occasionally, a grim warrior among them started half upright, grasping his tomahawk, as if to combat some vision of his disordered brain, but, unable to shake off the stupor from his senses, uniformly fell back into his former position.

The rangers crept nearer. As they bent their keen eyes along their well-tried rifles, each felt perfectly sure of his aim. They waited for the signal of Harmon, who was endeavoring to bring his long musket to bear upon the head of the most distant of the savages.

"Fire!" he at length exclaimed, as the sight of his piece interposed full and distinct between his eye and the wild scalp-lock of the Indian. "Fire, and rush on!"

The sharp voice of thirty rifles thrilled through the heart of the forest. There was a groan—a smothered cry—a wild and convulsive movement among the sleeping Indians; and all again was silent.

The rangers sprang forward with their clubbed muskets and hunting knives; but their work was done. The red men had gone to their last audit before the Great Spirit; and no sound was heard among them, save the gurgling of the hot blood from their lifeless bosoms.

They were left unburied on the place of their revelling,—a prey to the foul birds of the air, and the
ravenous beasts of the wilderness.   Their scalps
were borne homeward in triumph by the successful
rangers, whose children and grand-children shuddered, long after, at the thrilling narration of the midnight adventure.

THE WEIRD GATHERING.

[THE fearful delusion of Witchcraft was principally confined to the county of Essex, in Massachusetts—although there were instances of it in other portions of New-England. It was there that the evil had its most powerful work. It was like a heavy judgment from God—the visitation of an indescribable and unaccounted-for curse—the passing over of a shadow upon the mental atmosphere like that of a thunder-cloud upon the physical. The following story is founded on a passage in the singular works of Cotton Mather, where that learned divine informs us that at the dead of night, the "witches and prestigious spirits and demons," who persecuted, by means of their spells and incantations, the good people of Massachusetts Bay, were assembled together by the sound of a great trumpet. The place of the evil gathering was somewhere near Naumkeag, now Salem.]

A trumpet in the darkness blown—
　　A peal upon the air—
The church-yard answers to its tone
With boding shriek and wail and groan—
　　The dead are gliding there!

It rose upon the still midnight,
　　A summons long and clear—
The wakeful shuddered with affright—
The dreaming sleeper sprang upright,
　　And pressed his stunning ear.

The Indian, where his serpent eye
　　Beneath the green-wood shone,

Started, and tossed his arms on high,
And answered, with his own wild cry,
   The sky's unearthly tone.

The wild birds rose in startled flocks,
   As the long trumpet swelled;
And loudly from their old, grey rocks,
The gaunt, fierce wolf, and caverned fox
   In mutual terror yelled.

There is a wild and haunted glen,
   'Twixt Saugus and Naumkeag—
'Tis said of old that wizard-men
And demons to that spot have been
   To consecrate their league.

A fitting place for such as these—
   That small and sterile plain,
So girt about with tall, old trees
Which rock and groan in every breeze,
   Like spirits cursed with pain.

It was the witch's trysting place—
   The wizard's chosen ground,
Where the accursed of human race
With demons gathered, face to face,
   By the midnight trumpet's sound.

And there that night the trumpet rang,
   And rock and hill replied,
And down the glen strange shadows sprang.
Mortal and fiend—a wizard gang—
   Seen dimly side by side.

They gathered there from every land
   That sleepeth in the sun,—
They came with spell and charm in hand,
Waiting their Master's high command—
   Slaves to the Evil One!

From islands of the far-off seas—
   From Hecla's ice and flame—
From where the loud and savage breeze
Growls through the tall Norwegian trees,
   Seer, witch and wizard came!

And, from the sunny land of palms,
   The negro hag was there—
The Gree-gree, with his Obi charms—
The Indian, with his tattooed arms,
   And wild and streaming hair!

The Gipsey with her fierce, dark eyes,
   The worshipper of flame—
The searcher out of mysteries,

Above a human sacrifice—
    All—all—together came !

    *   *   *   *   *   *

Nay, look not down that lighted dell,
    Thou startled traveller!—
Thy christian eye should never dwell
On gaunt, grey witch and fiend of hell
    And evil Trumpeter !

But, the traveller turned him from his way,
    For he heard the revelling—
And saw the red light's wizard ray
Among the dark leafed branches play,
    Like an unholy thing.

He knelt him on the rocks, and cast,
    A fearful glance beneath,—
Wizard and hag before him passed,
Each wilder, fiercer than the last,—
    His heart grew cold as death !

He saw the dark-browed Trumpeter,
    In human shape was he;
And witch and fiend and sorcerer,
With shriek and laugh and curses, were
    Assembled at his knee.

And lo—beneath his straining glance,
  A light form stole along—
Free, as if moving to the dance,
He saw her fairy steps advance
  Towards the evil throng.

The light along her forehead played—
  A wan, unearthly glare;
Her cheek was pale beneath the shade
The wildness of her tresses made,
  Yet nought of fear was there!

Now God have mercy on thy brain,
  Thou stricken traveller!—
Look on thy victim once again,
Bethink thee of her wrongs and pain—
  Dost thou remember her?

The traveller smote his burning brow,
  For he saw the wronged one there—
He knew her by her forehead's snow,
And by her large, blue eye below,
  And by her wild, dark hair.

Slowly, yet firm she held her way,—
  The wizard's song grew still—
    3

The sorcerer left his elvish play,
And hideous imp and beldame grey
  Waited the stranger's will.

A voice came up that place of fear--
  The Trumpeter's hoarse tone--
"Speak—who art thou that comest here
With brow baptized and christian ear,
  Unsummoned and alone ?"

One moment—and a tremor shook
  Her light and graceful frame,--
It passed—and then her features took
A fiercer and a haughtier look,
  As thus her answer came : --

    "Spirits of evil--
      Workers of doom !
    Lo—to your revel,
      For vengeance I come !
    Vengeance on him
      Who hath blighted my fame,--
    Fill his cup to the brim
      With a curse without name !
    Let his false heart inherit
      The madness of mine,

And I yield ye my spirit,
    And bow at your shrine!"

A sound—a mingled laugh and yell,
    Went howling fierce and far—
A redder light shone through the dell,
As if the very gates of hell
    Swung suddenly ajar.

"Breathe then thy curse, thou daring one,"
    A low, deep voice replied—
"Whate'er thou askest shall be done,
The burthen of thy doom upon
    The false one shall abide."

The maiden stood erect—her brow
    Grew dark as those around her,
As burned upon her lip that vow
Which christian ear may never know,—
    And the dark fetter bound her!

Ay, there she stood—the holy Heaven
    Was looking down on her—
An Angel from her bright home driven—
A spirit lost and doomed and given
    To fiend and sorcerer!

And changed—how changed!—her aspect grew
  Fearful and elvish there;
The warm tinge from her cheek withdrew,
And one dark spot of blood-red hue
  Burned on her forehead fair.

Wild from her eye of madness shone
  The baleful fire within,
As, with a shrill and lifted tone
She made her fearful purpose known,
  Before the powers of Sin :

    " Let my curse be upon him—
      The faithless of heart !
    Let the smiles that have won him
      In frowning depart !—
    Let his last, cherished blossom
      Of sympathy die,
    And the hopes of his bosom
      In shadows go by !—
    Ay, curse him—but keep
      The poor boon of his breath.
    'Till he sigh for the sleep,
      And the quiet of death !
    Let a viewless one haunt him
      With whisper and jeer,

And an evil one daunt him
  With phantoms of fear!—
Be the fiend unforgiving
  That follows his tread;
Let him walk with the living—
  Yet gaze on the dead!"

She ceased.—The doomed one felt the spell
  Already on his brain;
He turned him from the wizard-dell;
He prayed to Heaven; he cursed at hell;—
  He wept--and all in vain.

The night was one of mortal fear;
  The morning rose to him,
Dark as the shroudings of a bier,
As if the blessed atmosphere,
  Like his own soul, was dim.

He passed among his fellow men,
  With wild and dreamy air,
For, whispering in his ear again
The horrors of the midnight glen,
  The demon found him there.

3*

And, when he would have knelt and prayed,
 Amidst his household band,
An unseen power his spirit stayed.
And on his moving lip was laid
 A hot and burning hand!

The lost one in the solitude
 Of dreams he gazed upon,
And, when the holy morning glowed,
Her dark eye shone—her wild hair flowed
 Between him and the sun!

His brain grew wild,—-and then he died :
 Yet, ere his heart grew cold,
To the gray priest, who at his side
The strength of prayer and blessing tried.
 His fearful tale was told.

  *   *   *   *   *   *

They've bound the witch with many a thong --
 The holy priest is near her ;
And ever as she moves along,
A murmur rises hoarse and strong
 From those who hate and fear her.

She's standing up for sacrifice,
 Beneath the gallows-tree ;—
The silent town beneath her lies,

Above her are the Summer skies---
   Far off--the quiet sea.

So young--so frail--so very fair--
   Why should the victim die?--
Look on her brow!--the red stain there
Burns underneath her tangled hair--
   And mark her fiery eye!

A thousand eyes are looking up
   In scorn and hate to her;--
A bony hand hath coiled the rope,
And yawns upon the green hill's slope
   The witch's sepulchre!

Ha! she hath spurned both priest and book---
   Her hand is tossed on high--
Her curse is loud,--she will not brook
The impatient crowd's abiding look---
   Hark!--how she shrieks to die!

Up--up--one struggle--all is done!
   One groan--the deed is wrought.
Wo--for the wronged and fallen one!--
Her corse is blackening in the sun--
   Her spirit--trace it not!

NOTE. — —"She's standing up for sacrifice,
               Beneath the gallows-tree."

The place of the execution of the witches and wizards of the neighborhood of Salem is a naked hill, which overlooks the town and harbor. The tree from which they were suspended, was standing a few years since, blasted and dead with years—the heart of the wood only visible, like a gaunt skeleton, blackened by exposure to sun and storm.

THE RATTLESNAKE HUNTER.*

"Until my ghastly tale is told
This heart within me burns."
Rime of the Ancient Mariner.

DURING a delightful excursion in the vicinity of the Green Mountains, a few years since, I had the good fortune to meet with a singular character, known in many parts of Vermont as the Rattlesnake Hunter, It was a warm, clear day of sunshine, in the middle of June that I saw him for the first time, while engaged in a mineralogical ramble among the hills. His head was bald, and his forehead was deeply marked with the strong lines of care and age. His form was wasted and meagre; and, but for the fiery vigor of his eye, he might have been supposed incapacitated by age and infirmities for even a slight exertion. Yet he hurried over the rude ledges of rock with a quick and almost youthful tread; and seemed earnestly

---

* The Rattlesnake's power of fascination was generally admitted by the early settlers of the Colonies. That this serpent has actually the mysterious faculty of *charming*, or fascinating the prey upon which it subsists, is still believed, and upon good authority. That this power extended to human beings has also been asserted,—and that the effect produced by the charm upon the senses of its victim, was substantially the same as that described in the story of "The Rattlesnake Hunter."

searching among the crevices and loose crags and stinted bushes around him. All at once, he started suddenly—drew himself back with a sort of shuddering recoil—and then smote fiercely with his staff upon the rock before him. Another, and another blow.—and he lifted the lithe and crushed form of a large Rattlesnake upon the end of his rod.

The old man's eye glistened but his lip trembled, as he looked steadfastly upon his yet writhing victim. "Another of the cursed race!" he muttered, between his clenched teeth, apparently unconscious of my presence.

I was now satisfied that the person before me was none other than the famous Rattlesnake Hunter. He was known throughout the neighborhood as an outcast, and a wanderer, obtaining a miserable subsistence from the casual charities of the people around him. His time was mostly spent among the rocks and rude hills, where his only object seemed to be the hunting out and destroying of the dreaded *Crotalus horridus*, or Rattlesnake. I immediately determined to satisfy my curiosity, which had been strangely excited by the remarkable appearance and behavior of the stranger; and for this purpose I approached him.

"Are there many of these reptiles in this vicinity?" I enquired, pointing to the crushed serpent.

"They are getting to be scarce," said the old man, lifting his slouched hat and wiping his bald brow; "I have known the time when you could hardly stir ten rods from your door in this part of the State without hearing their low, quick rattle at your side, or seeing their many-colored bodies coiling up in your path. But, as I said before, they are getting to be scarce—the infernal race will be extinct in a few years;—and thank God, I have myself been a considerable cause of their extermination."

"You must, of course, know the nature of these creatures perfectly well," said I. "Do you believe in their power of fascination or charming?"

The old man's countenance fell. There was a visible struggle of feeling within him: for his lip quivered, and he dashed his brown hand suddenly across his eyes, as if to conceal a tear. But quickly recovering himself, he answered in the low, deep voice of one about to reveal some horrible secret—

"I believe in the Rattlesnake's power of fascination as firmly as I believe in my own existence."

"Surely," said I, "you do not believe that they have power over human beings?"

"I do—I know it to be so!"—and the old man trembled as he spoke.—"You are a stranger to me," he said slowly, after scrutinizing my features for a moment,—"but if you will go down with me to the foot of this rock, in the shade there"—and he pointed to a group of leaning oaks that hung over the declivity—"I will tell you a strange and sad story of my own experience."

It may be supposed that I readily assented to this proposal. Bestowing one more blow on the rattlesnake, as if to be certain of his death, the old man descended the rocks with a rapidity, which would have endangered the neck of a less practiced hunter. After reaching the spot which he had pointed out, the Rattlesnake Hunter commenced his story in a manner which confirmed what I had previously heard of his education and intellectual strength.

"I was among the earliest settlers in this part of the country. I had just finished my education at the University of Harvard, when I was induced, by the flattering representations of some of the earlier pioneers into the wild lands beyond the Connecticut, to seek my fortune in the new settlements. My wife"— the old man's eye glistened an instant, and then a tear crossed his brown cheek—"my wife accompanied me, young and delicate and beautiful as she was, to this wild and rude country. I shall never forgive myself for bringing her hither—never. "Young man," he continued, "you look like one who could pity me.—

You shall see the image of the girl who followed me to the new country." And he unbound, as he spoke, a ribbon from his neck, with a small miniature attached to it.

It was that of a beautiful female. She might have been twenty years of age—but there was an almost childish expression in her countenance,—a softness—a delicacy, and a sweetness of smile, which I have seldom seen in the features of those who have tasted, even slightly, of the bitter waters of existence. The old man watched my countenance intently, as I surveyed the image of his early love. "She must have been very beautiful," I said, as I returned the picture.

"Beautiful!" he repeated, "you may well say so. But this avails nothing. I have a fearful story to tell: would to God I had not attempted it; but I will go on. My heart has been stretched too often on the rack of memory to suffer any new pang."

"We had resided in the new country nearly a year. Our settlements had increased rapidly; and the comforts and delicacies of life were beginning to be felt, after the weary privations, and severe trials to which we had been subjected. The red men were few and feeble, and did not molest us. The beasts of the forest and mountain were ferocious, but we suffered little from them. The only immediate danger to which we

4

were exposed resulted from the Rattlesnakes which infested our neighborhood. Three or four of our settlers were bitten by them, and died in terrible agonies. The Indians often told us frightful stories of this snake, and its powers of fascination, and although they were generally believed, yet for myself, I confess, I was rather amused than convinced by their marvellous legends.

"In one of my hunting excursions abroad, on a fine morning—it was just at this time of the year—I was accompanied by my wife. 'Twas a beautiful morning. The sunshine was warm, but the atmosphere was perfectly clear; and a fine breeze from the northwest shook the bright, green leaves which clothed to profusion the wreathing branches above us. I had left my companion for a short time, in pursuit of game; and in climbing a rugged ledge of rocks, interspersed with shrubs and dwarfish trees, I was startled by a quick, grating rattle. I looked forward. On the edge of a loosened rock lay a large Rattlesnake, coiling himself, as if for the deadly spring. He was within a few feet of me; and I paused for an instant to survey him. I know not why, but I stood still, and looked at the deadly serpent with a strange feeling of curiosity. Suddenly he unwound his coil, as if relenting from his purpose of hostility, and raising his head, he fixed his bright, fiery eye directly upon my own. A chilling and indescribable sensation totally different from any thing I had ever before experienced, followed this movement of the serpent; but I stood still, and gazed steadily and earnestly, for at that moment there was a visible change in the reptile.— His form seemed to grow larger, and his colors brighter. His body moved with a slow, almost imperceptible motion towards me, and a low hum of music came from him—or, at least, it sounded in my ear—a strange, sweet melody, faint as that which melts from the throat of the Humming-bird. Then the tints of his body deepened, and changed and glowed, like the changes of a beautiful kaleidoscope,— green, purple and gold, until I lost sight of the serpent entirely, and saw only wild and curiously woven circles of strange colors, quivering around me, like an atmosphere of rainbows. I seemed in the centre of a great prism—a world of mysterious colors;—and the tints varied and darkened and lighted up again around me; and the low music went on without ceasing, until my brain reeled; and fear, for the first time, came like a shadow over me. The new sensation gained upon me rapidly, and I could feel the cold sweat gushing from my brow. I had no certainty of danger in my mind—no definite ideas of peril—all

was vague and clouded, like the unaccountable terrors
of a dream,—and yet my limbs shook, and I fancied I
could feel the blood stiffening with cold as it passed
along my veins.   I would have given worlds to have
been able to tear myself from the spot—I even attempted to do so, but the body obeyed not the im-
pulse of the mind—not a muscle stirred; and I stood
still, as if my feet had grown to the solid rock, with
the infernal music of the tempter in my car, and the
baleful colorings of his enchantment before me.

Suddenly a new sound came on my ear—it was a
human voice—but it seemed strange and awful. Again
—again—but I stirred not; and then a white form
plunged before me, and grasped my arm.   The horrible spell was at once broken.   The strange colors
passed from before my vision.   The Rattlesnake was
coiling at my very feet, with glowing eyes and uplift-
ed fangs; and my wife was clinging in terror upon
me.   The next instant the serpent threw himself upon
us.   My wife was the victim!—The fatal fangs pierced
deeply into her hand; and her scream of agony, as
she staggered backward from me, told me the dreadful truth.

Then it was that a feeling of madness came upon
me; and when I saw the foul serpent stealing away
from his work of death, reckless of danger, I sprang

forward and crushed him under my feet, grinding him
in pieces upon the ragged rock. The groans of my
wife now recalled me to her side, and to the horrible
reality of her situation. There was a dark, livid spot
on her hand ; and it deepened into blackness as I led
her away. We were at a considerable distance from
any dwelling; and after wandering for a short time,
the pain of her wound became insupportable to my
wife, and she swooned away in my arms. Weak and
exhausted as I was, I had yet strength enough remaining to carry her to the nearest rivulet, and bathe her
brow in the cool water. She partially recovered, and
sat down upon the bank, while I supported her head
upon my bosom. Hour after hour passed away, and
none came near us,—and there—alone, in the great
wilderness, I watched over her, and prayed with her
—and she died !

The old man groaned audibly, as he uttered these
words ; and, as he clasped his long, bony hands over
his eyes, I could see the tears falling thickly through
his gaunt fingers. After a momentary struggle with
his feelings, he lifted his head once more, and there
was a fierce light in his eye as he spoke:

"But I have had my revenge. From that fatal moment I have felt myself fitted and set apart, by the terrible ordeal of affliction, to rid the place of my abode

4*

of its foulest curse. And I have well nigh succeeded. The fascinating demons are already few and powerless. Do not imagine," said he, earnestly regarding the somewhat equivocal expression of my countenance, " that I consider these creatures as serpents only—creeping serpents;—they are the servants of the fallen Angel--the immediate ministers of the infernal Gulf !"

*   *   *   *   *   *

Years have passed since my interview with the Rattlesnake Hunter: the place of his abode has changed —a beautiful village rises near the spot of our conference, and the grass of the church yard is green over the grave of the old Hunter. But his story is yet fixed upon my mind, and Time, like enamel, only burns deeper the first strong impression. It comes up before me like a vividly remembered dream, whose features are too horrible for reality.

METACOM.

[Metacom, or Philip, the chief of the Wampanoags, was the most powerful and sagacious Sachem who ever made war upon the English. He had all the qualities of a high statesman—a noble monarch, and a courageous warrior. The rude majesty of untamed and unchastened nature was never more boldly developed than in the character of Metacom. He had the elements of a giant mind—the unformed chaos of a world of intellect. He perilled his all in one vast enterprise—in one mighty effort to shake off the White Vampyre which was draining the life-blood of his people; and had his enemies been any other than the stern settlers of New-England, they must assuredly have fallen. The War of King Philip forms a dark page in the history of New-England.—It is red with blood,—with the blood of the strong man and the meek and beseeching woman, and the fair-haired child, and the cradled infant.]

RED as the banner which enshrouds
   The warrior-dead, when strife is done,
A broken mass of crimson clouds
   Hung over the departed sun.
The shadow of the western hill
Crept swiftly down, and darkly still,
As if a sullen wave of night
Were rushing on the pale twilight—
The forest-openings grew more dim,
   As glimpses of the arching blue
   And waking stars came softly through
The rifts of many a giant limb.
 Above the wet and tangled swamp
 White vapors gathered thick and damp,

And through their cloudy-curtaining
Flapped many a brown and dusky wing—
Pinions that fan the moonless dun,
But fold them at the rising sun !

Beneath the closing veil of night,
　And leafy bough and curling fog,
With his few warriors ranged in sight—
Scarred relics of his latest fight—
　Rested the fiery Wampanoag.
He leaned upon his loaded gun,
Warm with its recent work of death,
And, save the struggling of his breath
　That, slow and hard, and long-suppressed,
Shook the damp folds around his breast.
An eye, that was unused to scan
The sterner moods of that dark man,
Had deemed his tall and silent form,
With hidden passion fierce and warm,
With that fixed eye, as still and dark
As clouds which veil their lightning spark—
That of some forest-champion,
Whom sudden death had passed upon—
A giant frozen into stone !
Son of the throned Sachem !—Thou,
　The sternest of the forest kings,—

Shall the scorned pale-one trample now,
Unambushed on thy mountain's brow,
Yea, drive his vile and hated plough
   Among thy nation's holy things,
Crushing the warrior-skeleton
In scorn beneath his armed heel,
And not a hand be left to deal
A kindred vengeance fiercely back,
And cross in blood the Spoiler's track!

He started,—for a sudden shot
   Came booming through the forest-trees—
   The thunder of the fierce Yengeese:
It passed away, and injured not;
But, to the Sachem's brow it brought
The token of his lion thought.
He stood erect—his dark eye burned,
As if to meteor-brightness turned;
And o'er his forehead passed the frown
Of an archangel stricken down,
Ruined and lost, yet chainless still—
Weakened of power but strong of will!
It passed—a sudden tremor came
Like ague o'er his giant frame,—
It was not terror—he had stood
   For hours, with death in grim attendance,

When moccasins grew stiff with blood,
And through the clearing's midnight flame,
Dark, as a storm, the Pequod came,
   His red, right arm their strong dependence—
When thrilling through the forest gloom
The onset-cry of " Metacom !"
   Rang on the red and smoky air !—
No—it was agony which passed
Upon his soul—the strong man's last
   And fearful struggle with despair.

He turned him to his trustiest one—
The old and war-tried Annawon—
" Brother!"—The favored warrior stood
In hushed and listening attitude—
"This night the Vision-Spirit hath
   Unrolled the scroll of fate before me ;
And ere the sunrise cometh, Death
   Will wave his dusky pinion o'er me !
Nay, start not—well I know thy faith—
Thy weapon now may keep its sheath ;
But, when the bodeful morning breaks,
And the green forest widely wakes,
   Unto the roar of Yengeese thunder,
Then trusted brother, be it thine
To burst upon the foeman's line,

And rend his serried strength asunder.
Perchance thyself and yet a few
Of faithful ones may struggle through,
And, rallying on the wooded plain,
Strike deep for vengeance once again,
And offer up in Yengeese blood
An offering to the Indian's God."

Another shot—a sharp, quick yell—
  And then the stifled groan of pain,
Told that another red man fell,—
  And blazed a sudden light again
Across that kingly brow and eye,
Like lightning on a clouded sky,—
And a low growl, like that which thrills
The hunter of the Eastern hills,
  Burst through clenched teeth and rigid lip —
And, when the Monarch spoke again
His deep voice shook beneath its rein,
  As wrath and grief held fellowship.

" Brother ! methought when as but now
  I pondered on my nation's wrong,
With sadness on his shadowy brow
  My father's spirit passed along !
He pointed to the far south-west,

Where sunset's gold was growing dim,
And seemed to beckon me to him,
And to the forests of the blest!—
My father loved the Yengeese, when
They were but children, shelterless,
For his great spirit at distress
Melted to woman's tenderness—
Nor was it given him to know
That, children whom he cherished then,
Would rise at length, like armed men,
To work his people's overthrow.
Yet thus it is ;—the God, before
Whose awful shrine the pale ones bow,
Hath frowned upon, and given o'er
The red man to the stranger now !—
A few more moons—and there will be
No gathering to the council tree—
The scorched earth—the blackened log—
The naked bones of warriors slain,
Be the sole relics which remain
Of the once mighty Wampanoag !
The forests of our hunting-land,
With all their old and solemn green,
Will bow before the Spoiler's axe—
The plough displace the hunter's tracks,

And the tall Yengeese altar stand
   Where the Great Spirit's shrine hath been!

Yet, brother, from this awful hour
   The dying curse of Metacom
Shall linger with abiding power
   Upon the spoilers of my home.
   The fearful veil of things to come,
   By Kitchtan's hand is lifted from
The shadows of the embryo years;
   And I can see more clearly through
Than ever visioned Powwah did,
For all the future comes unbid
   Yet welcome to my tranced view,
As battle-yell to warrior-ears!
From stream and lake and hunting-hill,
   Our tribes may vanish like a dream,
   And even my dark curse may seem
Like idle winds when Heaven is still—
   No bodeful harbinger of ill,
Bu,t fiercer than the downright thunder,
When yawns the mountain-rock asunder,
And riven pine and knotted oak
Are reeling to the fearful stroke,
   That curse shall work its master's will!
The bed of yon blue mountain stream
     5

Shall pour a darker tide than rain—
The sea shall catch its blood-red stain,
And broadly on its banks shall gleam
    The steel of those who should be brothers
Yea—those whom one fond parent nursed
Shall meet in strife, like fiends accursed—
And trample down the once loved form,
While yet with breathing passion warm,
    As fiercely as they would another's !"

The morning star sat dimly on
The lighted eastern horizon—
The deadly glare of levelled gun
    Came streaking through the twilight haze
    And naked to its reddest blaze,
A hundred warriors sprang in view—
    One dark red arm was tossed on high—
One giant shout came hoarsely through
    The clangour and the charging cry,
Just as across the scattering gloom,
Red as the naked hand of Doom,
    The Yengeese volley hurtled by—
The arm—the voice of Metacom !—
    One piercing shriek—one vengeful yell,
Sent like an arrow to the sky,
    Told when the hunter-monarch fell !

NOTES.

"Unambushed on thy mountain's brow."

Mount Hope—the residence of King Philip, or Metacom. Near this place, on the 12th of August, 1676, Philip fought his last battle, and fell by the fire of the English. It was a proud day for New-England. It sealed forever the destiny of the Indian; and established the security of the Colonies. It is supposed that Metacom had gathered In the outset a body of fighting men, 3000 strong. These had, for the most part, been scattered and destroyed by battle and famine; and the fall of their leader was the precursor of the total overthrow of the remainder. New-England suffered severely in this war. 600 of her young men—her flower and her strength—perished in battle.

"The thunder of the fierce Yengeese."

The Indian name of the English was Yingeese or Yengeese.

"He turned him to his trustiest one—
The old and war-tried Annawon."

Annawon, or Artnawon, was Philip's latest and bravest Captain. When, on the morning of the fight at Mount Hope, Metacom fell, in an attempt to escape from the swamp in which he had been enclosed by the English, Annawon, at the head of a handful of brave men, defended himself through the day. His terrific war-cry rang with almost super-human loudness through the swamp, when he saw his Monarch fall, amidst the exultation of his enemies.

"My father loved the Yengeese, when
They were but children, shelterless."

Massasoit was the father of Metacom. He was the fast friend of the white men. Soon after the landing of the Pilgrims at Plymouth, they were astonished at seeing a tall and noble-looking Indian walk into their little town, and salute them with "Welcome Englishmen!" It was Massasoit.

THE MURDERED LADY.

[In the 17th century, when the sea-robbers were ravaging the commerce of Spain, a vessel of that nation was brought into the port of Marblehead, by a pirate brig. For the better security of its rich cargo, the unfortunate crew were barbarously massacred. A lady was brought on shore by the pirates, and murdered, and afterwards buried in a deep glen or valley, at a little distance from the village. The few inhabitants of the place, at that early period of its history, were unable to offer any resistance to the fierce and well armed buccaneers. They heard the shrieks of the unfortunate lady, mingled with the savage shouts of her murderers, but could afford her no succor. There is a tradition among some of the old inhabitants of Marblehead, that these sounds have been heard ever since, at intervals of two or three years, in the valley where the lady was buried.]

A dark-hulled brig at anchor rides,
　Within the still and moonlight bay,
And round its black, portentous sides
　The waves like living creatures play !—
And close at hand a tall ship lies—
　A voyager from the Spanish Main,
Laden with gold and merchandize—
　She'll ne'er return again!

The fisher in his seaward skiff,
　Creeps stealthily along the shore,
Within the shadow of the cliff,
　Where keel had never ploughed before ;

He turns him from that stranger bark,
  And hurries down the silver bay,
Where, like a demon still and dark,
  She watches o'er her prey.

     *   *   *   *   *

The midnight came.—A dash of oars
  Broke on the ocean-stillness then,
And swept towards the rocky shores,
  The fierce wild forms of outlawed men ;—
The tenants of that fearful ship,
  Grouped strangely in the pale moon-light—
Dark, iron brow and bearded lip,
  Ghastly with storm and fight.

They reach the shore,—but who is she—
  The white-robed one they bear along ?
She shrieks—she struggles to be free—
  God shield that gentle one from wrong ;
It may not be,—those pirate men,
  Along the hushed, deserted street,
Have borne her to a narrow glen,
  Scarce trod by human feet.

     *   *   *   *   *

And there the ruffians murdered her,
  When not an eye, save Heaven's beheld;
       5 *

Ask of the shuddering villager,
　　What sounds upon the night air swelled
Woman's long shriek of mortal fear—
　　Her wild appeal to hearts of stone,
The oath—the taunt—the brutal jeer—
　　The pistol-shot—the groan !

With shout and jest and losel song,
　　From savage tongues which knew no rein,
The stained with murder passed along,
　　And sought their ocean-home again ;—
And all the night their revel came
　　In hoarse and sullen murmurs on,—
A yell rang up—a burst of flame—
　　The Spanish Ship was gone !

The morning light came red and fast
　　Along the still and blushing sea ;
The phantoms of the night had passed—
　　That ocean-robber—where was she !—
Her sails were reaching from the wind,
　　Her crimson banner-folds were stirred ;
And ever and anon behind,
　　Her shouting crew were heard.

Then came the village-dwellers forth,
  And sought with fear the fatal glen ;—
The stain of blood—the trampled earth
  Told where the deed of death had been.
They found a grave—a new-made one—
  With bloody sabres hollowed out,
And shadowed from the searching sun,
  By tall trees round about.

They left the hapless stranger there ;
  They knew her sleep would be as well,
As if the priest had poured his prayer
  Above her—with the funeral-bell.
The few poor rites which man can pay,
  Are felt not by the lonely sleeper ;
The deaf, unconscious ear of clay
  Heeds not the living weeper.

They tell a tale—those sea-worn men,
  Who dwell along that rocky coast,
Of sights and sounds within the glen,
  Of midnight shriek and gliding ghost.
And oh ! if ever from their chill
  And dreamless sleep, the dead arise,
That victim of unhallowed ill
  Might wake to human eyes !

They say that often when the morn,
   Is struggling with the gloomy even ;
And over moon and star is drawn
   The curtain of a clouded heaven—
Strange sounds swell up the narrow glen,
   As if that robber-crew were there—
The hellish laugh—the shouts of men—
   And woman's dying prayer !

THE UNQUIET SLEEPER.

[Some fifty or sixty years since, an inhabitant of ———, N. H. was found dead at a little distance from his dwelling, which he left in the morning in perfect health. There is a story prevalent among the people of the neighborhood, that, on the evening of the day on which he was found dead, strange cries are annually heard to issue from his grave! I have conversed with some who really supposed they had heard them, in the dead of the night, rising fearfully on the Autumn wind. They represented the sounds to be of a most appalling and unearthly nature. Idle as this story may be, it is made the subject of the following lines:]

THE Hunter went forth with his dog and gun,
In the earliest glow of the golden sun ;—
The trees of the forest bent over his way,
In the changeful colours of Autumn gay ;
For a frost had fallen the night before,
On the quiet greenness which Nature wore.

A bitter frost !—for the night was chill,
And starry and dark, and the wind was still,
And so when the sun looked out on the hills,
On the stricken woods and the frosted rills,
The unvaried green of the landscape fled,
And a wild, rich robe was given instead.

We know not whither the Hunter went,
Or how the last of his days was spent ;

For the noon drew nigh—but he came not back,
Weary and faint from his forest track ;
And his wife sat down to her frugal board,
Beside the empty seat of her lord.;

And the day passed on, and the sun came down
To the hills of the west, like an angel's crown,
The shadows lengthened from wood and hill,
The mist crept up from the meadow-rill,
'Till the broad sun sank, and the red light rolled
All over the west, like a wave of gold !

Yet he came not back—though the stars gave forth
Their wizard light to the silent Earth ;—
And his wife looked out from the lattice dim
Ir the earnest manner of fear for him ;
And his fair-haired child on the door-stone stood
To welcome his father back from the wood !

He came not back !—yet they found him soon,
In the burning light of the morrow's noon,
In the fixed and visionless sleep of death,
Where the red leaves fell at the soft wind's breath ;
And the dog whose step in the chase was fleet,
Crouched silent and sad at the Hunter's feet.

He slept in death ;—but his sleep was one,
Which his neighbors shuddered to look upon ;
For his brow was black, and his open eye
Was red with the sign of agony :
And they thought, as they gazed on his features grim,
That an evil deed had been done on him.

They buried him where his fathers laid,
By the mossy mounds in the grave-yard shade,
Yet whispers of doubt passed over the dead,
And beldames muttered while prayers were said ;
And the hand of the sexton shook as he pressed
The damp earth down on the Hunter's breast.

The seasons passed —and the Autumn rain
And the coloured forest returned again ;
'Twas the very eve that the Hunter died,
The winds wail'd over the bare hill-side,
And the wreathing limbs of the forest shook
Their red leaves over the swollen brook.

There came a sound on the night-air then,
Like a spirit-shriek, to the homes of men,
And louder and shriller it rose again
Like the fearful cry of the mad with pain ;

And trembled alike the timid and brave,
For they knew that it came from the Hunter's grave!

And every year, when Autumn flings
Its beautiful robe on created things,
When Piscataqua's tide is turbid with rain
And Cocheco's woods are yellow again,
That cry is heard from the grave-yard earth,
Like the howl of a demon struggling forth!

THE HAUNTED HOUSE.

THE beautiful river, which retains its Indian name of Merrimack, winds through a country of almost romantic beauty. The last twenty miles of its course in particular, are unsurpassed in quiet and rich scenery, by any river in the United States. There are indeed, no bold and ragged cliffs, like the Highlands of the Hudson, to cast their grim shadows on the water —no blue and lofty mountains, piercing into the thin atmosphere, and wrapping about their rocky proportions the mists of valley and river—but there are luxuriant fields and pleasant villages, and white church-spires, gleaming through the green foliage of oak and elm—and wide forests of Nature's richest coloring, and green hills sloping smoothly and gracefully to the margin of the clear, bright stream, which moves onward to the Ocean, as lightly and gracefully as the moving of a cloud at sunset, when the light wind which propels the ærial voyager is unfelt on earth.

It was on the margin of this stream, during the early times of Massachusetts, that a stranger—a foreigner of considerable fortune—took up his residence.

6

He had a house, constructed from a model of his own which, for elegance and convenience, far surpassed the rude and simple tenements of his neighbors ; and he had a small farm, or rather garden, which he seemed to cultivate for amusement, rather than from any absolute necessity of labor. He had no family, save a daughter—an interesting girl of sixteen.

Near the dwelling of Adam McOrne—for such was the stranger's name—lived old Alice Knight—a woman, known throughout the whole valley of the river, from Plum Island to the residence of the Sachem Passaconaway, on the Nashua,—as one under an evil influence—an ill-tempered and malignant old woman —who was seriously suspected of dealing with the Prince of Darkness. Many of her neighbors were ready to make oath that they had been haunted by old Alice, in the shape of a black cat—that she had taken off the wheels of their hay-carts and frozen down their sled-runners, when the team was in full motion —that she had bewitched their swine, and rendered their cattle unruly—nay, more than one good wife averred, that she had bewitched their churns and prevented the butter from forming ; and that they could expel her in no other way, than by heating a horse-nail and casting it into the cream. Moreover, they asserted that when this method of exorcism was resorted to, they invariably learned, soon after, that goodwife Alice was suffering under some unknown indisposition. In short, it would be idle to attempt a description of the almost innumerable feats of witchcraft ascribed to the withered and decrepid Alice.

Her exterior was indeed well calculated to favor the idea of her supernatural qualifications. She had the long, blue and skinny finger—the elvish locks of gray and straggling hair—the hooked nose, and the long, upturned chin, which seemed perpetually to threaten its nasal neighbor—the blue lips drawn around a mouth, garnished with two or three unearthly-looking fangs—the bleared and sunken eye—the bowed and attenuated form—and the limping gait, as if the invisible fetters of the Evil One were actually clogging the footsteps of his servant. Then, too, she was poor —poor as the genius of poverty itself—she had no relatives about her—no friends—her hand was against every man, and every man's hand was against her.

Setting the question of her powers of witchcraft aside, Alice Knight was actually an evil-hearted woman. Whether the suspicions and the taunts of her neighbors had aroused into action those evil passions which slumber in the seldom-visited depths of the human heart—or, whether the mortifications of poverty and dependence had changed and perverted her proud spirit—certain it was, that she took advantage of the credulity and fears of her neighbors. When they in the least offended her, she turned upon them with the fierce malison of an enraged Pythoness, and prophesied darkly of some unknown and indescribable evil about to befall them. And, consequently, if any evil *did* befall them in the space of a twelve-month afterward, another mark was added to the already black list of iniquities, which was accredited to the ill-favored Alice.

With all her fierce and deep-rooted hatred of the human species—one solitary affection—one feeling of kindness, yet lingered in the bosom of Alice Knight. Her son—a young man of twenty-five—her only child —seemed to form the sole and last link of the chain which had once bound her to humanity. Her love of him partook of the fierce passions of her nature—it was wild, ungovernable, and strong as her hate itself.

Gilbert Knight inherited little from his mother, save a portion of her indomitable pride and fierce temperament. He had been a seaman—had visited many of the old lands, and had returned again to his birth-place—a grown up man—with a sun-burned cheek—a fine and noble figure, and a countenance rude and forbidding, yet marked with a character of intellect and conscious power. He had little inter-

course with his mother—he refused even to reside in
the same dwelling with her—and yet, when in her
presence, he was respectful, and even indulgent to her
singular disposition and unsocial habits. He had no
communion with the inhabitants of his native town—
but, stern, unsocial and gloomy, he held himself apart
from the sympathies and fellowship of men, with
whom indeed, he had few feelings in common.

Mary, the daughter of Adam McOrne, seemed alone
to engage the attention of Gilbert Knight. She was
young, beautiful, and, considering the condition of the
country, well-educated. She naturally felt herself
superior to the rude and hard-featured youth around
her—she had tasted enough of the sentiment, and received enough of the polish of education, to raise her
ideas, at least, above the ignorant and unlettered rus-
tics, who sought her favor.

Despised and spurned at, as the mother of Gilbert
Knight was, still her son always commanded respect.
There was something in the dignity of his manner,
and the fierce flash of his dark eye, which had a powerful influence on all in his presence. Then, too, it
was remembered that his father was a man of intellect and family—that he was once wealthy—and had
suddenly met with reverses of fortune. These con-
siderations gave Gilbert Knight no little consequence

5*

in his native village; and Adam McOrne, who ridiculed the idea of witches and witchcraft, received the occasional visits of Gilbert with as much cordiality as if his mother had never been suspected of evil doings. He was pleased with the frank, bold bearing of the sailor; and with his evident preference of his dwelling, above that of his neighbors—never so much as dreaming, that the visits of Gilbert were paid to any other than himself..

It was a cold, dark night of Autumn, that Gilbert, after leaving the hospitable fire-side of McOrne, directed his steps to the rude and lonely dwelling of his mother. He found the old woman alone;—a few sticks of ignited wood cast a faint light upon the dismal apartment—and an old and blear-eyed cat was at her side, gazing earnestly at her unseemly countenance.

"Mother," said Gilbert, seating himself, "'tis idle—'tis worse than folly to dream of executing our project. Mary McOrne will never be my wife."

"Ha!" exclaimed Alice, fixing her hollow eye upon her son—"Have I not told you that it *should* be so, and *must* be? You have lost your courage; you have become weaker than a woman, Gilbert. I tell you that Mary McOrne loves you, as deeply, as passionately as ever man was loved by woman!"

Gilbert started. "I do believe she loves me," he said at length, "but she will never be my wife. She dreads an alliance with our family. She has said so —she has this night solemnly averred that she had rather die at once, than become the daughter-in-law of—of"—Gilbert hesitated.

"Of a witch!" shrieked Alice, in a voice so loud and shrill that it even startled the practiced ear of Gilbert. "'Tis well—I will not be stigmatised as a witch with impunity. That haughty Scotchman and his impudent brat of a daughter shall learn that Alice Knight is not to be insulted in this manner! Gilbert, you shall marry her, or she shall die accursed!"

"Mother!" said Gilbert, rising and fixing his dark eye keenly on that of his mother—"I understand your threat; and I warn you to beware. Practice your infernal tricks upon others as you please—but Mary McOrne is too pure and sacred for such unhallowed dealing; and as you dread the curses of your son, let her not be molested."

He turned away as he ceased speaking, and instantly left the dwelling. He had seen little of his mother for many years—he knew her disposition but imperfectly; and, while in public he ridiculed the idea of her supernatural powers, he yet felt an awe— a fear in her presence—a certainty that she was not

like those around her. He knew that the breath of
her displeasure operated to appearance like a curse—
that she *did*, either by natural cunning, or supernatural power, mysteriously distress and perplex her
neighbors. He saw that her proud spirit had been
touched ; and that she meditated evil against McOrne
and his daughter. The latter, Gilbert really loved—
as deeply and devotedly as such a rude spirit could
love ; and he shuddered at the idea of her subjection
to the arts of his mother. He therefore resolved to
press his suit once more, and endeavor to overcome
the objections which the girl had raised ; and, in the
event of his failure to do so, to protect her from the
wrath of his mother.

But Mary McOrne—much as she loved the dark-
eyed stranger, and his tales of peril and shipwreck in
other climes—could not associate herself with the son
of a witch—the only surviving offspring of a woman,
whom she verily believed to be the bond slave of the
Tempter. And so she strove with the strong feeling
of affection within her—and Gilbert Knight was re-
jected.

A short time after, the tenants of the dwelling of
McOrne were alarmed by strange sounds and unusu-
sual appearances. In the dead of the night they
would hear heavy footsteps ascending the stair-case,

with the clank of a chain—and groans issued from the unoccupied rooms of the building. The doors were mysteriously opened, after having been carefully secured—the curtains of the beds of McOrne and his daughter were drawn aside by an unseen hand; and low whispers of blasphemy and licentiousness, which a spirit of evil, could only have suggested, were breathed, as it were, into their very ears. The servants—a male and female—alike complained of preternatural visitations and unseemly visions. They were disturbed in their daily avocations—the implements of household labor were snatched away by an invisible hand—they saw strange lights in the neighborhood of the dwelling. They heard an unearthly music in the chimney; and saw the furniture of the room dancing about, as if moving to the infernal melody. In short, the fact was soon established, beyond the interposition of a doubt, that *the house was haunted.*

The days of faery are over. The tale of enchantment—the legend of ghostly power—of unearthly warning and supernatural visitation, have lost their hold on the minds of the great multitude. People sleep quietly where they are placed—no matter by what means they have reached the end of their jour-

ney—and there is an end to the church-yard rambles
of discontented ghosts—

> ————————"That creep
> From out the places where they sleep—
> To publish forth some hidden sin,
> Or drink the ghastly moonshine in," —

And as for witches, the race is extinct—or, if a few
yet remain, they are a miserable libel upon the dia-
bolical reputation of those who figured in the days of
Paris and Mather. Haunted houses are getting to be
novelties—and corpse-lights and apparitions and unearthly noises, and signs and omens and wonders, are
no longer troublesome. Ours is a matter-of-fact age
—an age of steam and railway and McAdamization
and labor-saving machinery—the poetry of Time has
gone by forever, and we have only the sober prose
left us.

Among the superstitions of our ancestors, that of
Haunted Houses is not the least remarkable. There
is scarcely a town or village in New-England which
has not, at some period or other of its history, had
one or more of these ill-fated mansions. They were
generally old, decayed buildings—untenanted, save
by the imaginary demons, who there held their midnight revels. But there are many instances of " prestigious spirits" who were impudent enough to locate

themselves in houses, where the hearth-stone had not
yet grown cold—where the big bible yet lay on the
parlor-table ; and where, over Indian-pudding and
pumpkin-pie, the good man of the mansion always
craved a blessing; where the big arm chair was always officiously placed for the minister of the parish,
whenever he favored the family with the light of his
countenance ; and where the good lady taught her
children the Catechism every Saturday evening.
This was indeed, a bold act of effrontery on the part
of the Powers of Evil, yet it was accounted for on the
ground, that good men and true were sometimes given
over to the buffetings of the enemy, of which fact, the
case of Job was considered ample proof.

The visitations to the house of McOrne became
more frequent and more terrific. The unfortunate
Mary suffered severely. She fully believed in the supernatural character of the sights and sounds which
alarmed her ; and she looked upon old Alice Knight
as the author : especially after hearing a whisper in
her ear, in the darkness of midnight, that, unless she
married Gilbert Knight she should be haunted as long
as she lived. As for the father, he battled long and
manfully with the fears which were strengthened day
by day—he laughed at the strange noises which filled
h is mansion, and ridiculed the fears of his daughter

—but it was easy to see that his strong mind was shaken by the controlling superstitions of the time; and he yielded slowly to the belief, which had now extended itself through the neighborhood, that his dwelling was under the immediate influence of demoniac agency.

Many were the experiments tried throughout the neighborhood for the discovery of the witch. The old, experienced grand-mothers gathered together almost every evening for consultation, and divers and multiform were the plans devised for counteracting the designs of Satan. All admitted that Alice Knight must be the witch, but unfortunately there was no positive proof of the fact. All the charms and forms of exorcism which were then believed to be potent weapons for the overthrowing of the powers of Wickedness having failed, it was finally settled among the good ladies that the minister of the parish could alone drive the evil spirits from the dwelling of their neighbor. But Adam McOrne was a sinful man ; and his oaths had been louder than his prayers on this trying occasion : and, when it was proposed to him to invite the godly parson to his house, for the purpose of laying the spirits that troubled it, he swore fiercely, that rather than have his threshold darkened by the puritan priest, he would see his dwelling converted into the Devil's ball-room, and thronged with all the evil spirits on the face of the earth or beneath it. And, with shaking heads and prophetic visages, the good women left the perverse Scotchman to his fate.

Notwithstanding his bold exterior, the heart of Adam McOrne was daily failing within him. The wild, nursery tales of his childhood came back to him with painful distinctness—and the bogle and kelpie and dwarfish Brownie of his native land, rose fearfully before his imagination. His evenings were lonely and long; and he resolved to invite Gilbert Knight—the fierce sailor, who feared neither man nor fiend—to take up his residence with him : in the firm belief that no power, human or super-human, could shake the nerves of a man, who had wrestled with the tempest upon every sea; and who had braved death in the red battle, when his shattered deck was slippery with blood and piled with human corses.

Gilbert obeyed the summons of McOrne with pleasure. He had heard the strange stories of the haunted mansion, which were upon every lip in the vicinity ; and he felt perfectly convinced that his mother was employed in disturbing the domestic quiet of the Scotchman and his daughter—whether by natural means, or othwise, he knew not. But he knew her revengeful disposition, and he feared, that unless

6

her schemes were boldly interfered with, she would
succeed in irreparably injuring the health and minds
of her victims. Besides, he trusted that, should he
succeed in accomplishing his purpose and laying the
evil spirits of the mansion, he should effectually se-
cure to himself the gratitude of both father and daughter.

Gilbert was received with much cordiality by Adam McOrne. "Ye may weel ken," said the old gentleman, "that I am no the least afeared o' a' this
clishmaclaver, o' evil speerits, or deils or witch-hags;
but my daughter, puir lassie, she's in an awsome way
—a' the time shakin' wi' fear o' wraiths and witches
and sic like ill-faured cattle." And Adam McOrne
made an endeavor to look unconcerned and resolute
in the presence of his guest, as he thus disclaimed any
feeling of alarm on his own part. He could not
bear that the bold sailor should look upon his weakness.

Even Mary McOrne welcomed the presence of her
discarded lover. Yet, while she clung to him as to
her only protector, she shuddered at the thought that
Gilbert was the son of her evil tormentor—nay more,
the horrible suspicion would at times steal over her
that he had himself prompted his wicked parent to
haunt her and terrify her into an acquiescence with

his wishes. But, when she heard his frank and manly proposal to watch all night in a chamber, where the strange sights and sounds were most frequent, she could not but trust that her suspicion was ill-founded, and that in Gilbert Knight she should find a friend and a protector.

Adam McOrne, secretly overjoyed at the idea of having a sentinel in his dwelling, ordered a fire to be kindled in the suspected chamber; and placing a decanter of spirits on the table, he bade his guest good night, and left him to the loneliness of the haunted apartment.

It matters not now what thoughts passed through the mind of Gilbert, as he sat silent and alone, gazing on the glowing embers before him. That his mother was engaged in a strange and dark purpose, in regard to the family of McOrne, he was fully convinced—and he resolved to unravel the mystery of her midnight adventures, and relieve the feelings of the Scotchman and his daughter—even, although in so doing he should implicate his own mother, in guilty and malicious designs.

The old family clock struck one. At that moment a deep groan sounded fearfully through the room.— Gilbert rose to his feet and listened earnestly. It seemed to proceed from the room beneath him; and it was repeated several times, until it died away, like the last murmurs of one in the agonies of death. In a few moments he heard footsteps on the stair case ascending to a long, narrow passage at its head, which communicated with his apartment.

"I will know the cause of this," said Gilbert, mentally, as he threw open the door, and sprang into the passage. A figure attempted to glide past him, appareled in white, uttering, as it did so, a deep and hollow groan.

"Mortal or devil!" shouted Gilbert, springing forward and grasping the figure by the arm—"you go no further. Speak, witch, ghost, whatever you are— declare your errand!"

The figure struggled violently, but the iron grasp of Gilbert remained unshaken. At that moment the hurried voice of the old Scotchman sounded through the passage.

"Haud weel, haud weel, my braw lad; dinna let go your grip—in God's name haud weel!"

"Let me go," said the figure in a hoarse whisper— "Let me go, or you are a dead man!" Gilbert retained his hold, and endeavored to discover by the dim light which streamed from his apartment, the countenance of the speaker.

"Die, then, unnatural wretch!" shrieked the derected Alice, snatching a knife from her bosom, and aiming a furious stab at her son. Gilbert pressed his hand to his side, and staggered backward, exclaiming, as the features of his mother, now fully revealed, glared madly upon him—

"Woman, you have murdered your son!"

The knife dropped from the hand of Alice, and with a loud and almost demoniac shriek, she sprang down the stair case and vanished like a spectre.

Adam McOrne hurried forward, the moment he saw the white figure disappear, and followed Gilbert into his apartment. "Are ye hurt?—are ye wraith-smitten?" asked the Scotchman; and then, as his eye fell on the bloodied dress of Gilbert, he exclaimed— "Waes me—ye are a' streakit wi' bluid—ye are a dead man!"

Gilbert felt that his wound was severe, but with his usual presence of mind, he gave such directions to McOrne and his daughter, as to enable them to prevent the rapid effusion of blood, while a servant was despatched for the nearest physician. Mary McOrne seemed to forget the weakness of her sex, while she ministered to her wounded lover with a quick eye and a skillful hand. It is on occasions like this—when even the strong nerves of manhood are shaken—that the feeble hand of woman is often most efficient. In

7*

the hour of excitement and turmoil, the spirit of man
ly daring may blaze out, with sudden and terrible
power—but in the deep trials of suffering humanity—
in the watchings by the bed of affliction—then it is
that the courage of woman predominates—the very
excess of her sympathy sustains her.

The arrival of the physician dissipated in some de-
gree the fears of McOrne and his daughter. The
wound of Gilbert was not considered as dangerous ;
and he was assured that a few days of confinement
would be the only ill consequence resulting from it.
The kind hearted Scotchman and his kinder hearted
daughter watched by his bed until morning, at which
time Gilbert was enabled to explain the singular cir-
cumstances of the night ; and at the same time he expressed a wish that McOrne should visit the dwelling
of his mother, who, he feared would resort to some
violence upon herself, in the belief that she had, in
her frantic passion, murdered her son.

Adam McOrne, convinced by the narration of Gilbert that human ingenuity and malice, instead of demoniac agency, had disturbed his dwelling, sallied
out early in the morning to the rude and crazy dwelling of his tormentor.

He found the door open—and on entering, the first
object that met his view was the form of Alice Knight,

lying on the floor, insensible and motionless. He
spoke to her, but she answered not—he lifted her arm,
and it fell back with a dead weight upon her side.—
She was dead—whether by terror or suicide, he knew
not. "Ugh!" said Adam McOrne, in relating the
discovery—"there she was—an ill-faured creature—
a' cauld and ghaistly, lookin' for a' the world as if she
wad hae thankit any Christian soul to hae gie'n her a
decent burial."

She was buried the next day in the small garden
adjoining her dwelling, for the good people of the
neighborhood could not endure the idea of her repo-
sing in their own quiet grave-yard. The minister of
the parish indeed attended her funeral, and made a
few general remarks upon the enormity of witchcraft
and the exceeding craftiness of the great necromancer
and magician, who had ensnared the soul of the ill-
fated Alice—but when he ventured to pray for the re-
pose of the unhappy woman, more than one of his
hearers shook their heads, in the belief that even their
own goodly minister had no right to interfere with
the acknowledged property of the Enemy.

It is said that Alice did not sleep peaceably, nath-
less the prayers of the minister. Her house was
often lighted up in the dead of the night, until

"Through ilka bore the flames were glancing."

and the wild and unearthly figure of the old woman herself, crossed more than once the paths of the good people of the neighborhood. At least, such is the story, and it is not our present purpose to dispute it.

The manner in which old Alice contrived to perplex the Scotchman and his daughter, was at length revealed by the disclosures of the servants of the family. They had been persuaded by the old woman to aid her in the strange transactions—partly from an innate love of mischief, and partly from a pique against the worthy Scotchman, whose irritable temperament had more than once discovered itself in the unceremonious collision of his cane with the heads and shoulders of his domestics.

Gilbert recovered rapidly of his wound : and a few months after, the house, which had been given over to the evil powers, as the revelling-place of demons, was brilliantly illuminated for a merry bridal. And the rough, bold sailor, as the husband of Mary Mc-Orne, settled down into a quiet, industrious and sober-minded citizen. Adam McOrne lived to a good old age, stoutly denying to the last that he had ever admitted the idea of witchcraft, and laughing, heartily as before, at the superstitions and credulity of his neighbors.

Note.—The preceding story is founded on a passage in the writings of Dr. Mather. "In 1679 a house," says the Doctor, "in Newbury, (on the Merrimack,) was infested with demons in a most horrid manner." Here follows a long and curious recital of the infernal doings of the ill-natured spirits. The same story is recorded on the records of the court at Salem, where a seaman, by the name of Powell, was tried for witchcraft, on the ground that he had been able to put to flight the demons of the haunted house, by means of the black art—or astrology.

THE SPECTRE WARRIORS.

[In 1692, the Garrison at Gloucester was alarmed by the appearance of several Indian warriors, some of whom advanced even unto the walls of the Garrison. They were repeatedly fired upon at the distance of a few yards, by the best marksmen, and, although the shot always seemed to take effect; and the strange Indians frequently fell as if mortally wounded, they always passed off in the end, unharmed. These invulnerable visitants continued for the space of three weeks to alarm and distress the Garrison.

Cotton Mather, in describing this circumstance, says:—"This inexplicable war might have some of its original among the Indians, whose Chief Sagamores are well known unto some of our captives, to have been horrid sorcerers, and hellish conjurers, such as conversed with Demons.—*Magnalia, Book 7, Article 18.*]

"AWAY to your arms ! for the foemen are here—
The yell of the red man is loud on the ear !
On—on to the garrison—soldiers away,
The moccasin's track shall be bloody to day."

The fortress is reached—they have taken their stand—
With war-knife in girdle, and rifle in hand ;—
Their wives are behind them—the savage before—
Will the puritan fail at his hearth-stone and door ?

There's a yell in the forest—unearthly and dread,
Like the shriek of a fiend o'er the place of the dead—
Again—how it swells through the forest afar—
Have the tribes of the fallen uprisen to war ?

Ha—look!—they are coming—not cautious and slow
In the serpent-like mood of the blood-seeking foe—
Nor stealing in shadow nor hiding in grass,
But tall, and uprightly and sternly they pass.

"Be ready!"—the watchword has passed on the wall,
The maidens have shrunk to the innermost hall—
The rifles are levelled—each head is bowed low—
Each eye fixes steady—God pity the foe!

They are closely at hand!—Ha! the red flash has broke
From the garrisoned wall through a curtain of smoke,
There's a yell from the dying—that aiming was true—
The red-man no more shall his hunting pursue!

Look—look to the earth, as the smoke rolls away,
Do the dying and dead on the green herbage lay?
What mean those wild glances? no slaughter is there—
The red-man has gone like the mist on the air!

Unharmed, as the bodiless air, he has gone
From the war-knife's edge and the ranger's long gun,
And the Puritan-warrior has turned him away
From the weapons of war, and is kneeling to pray!

He fears that the Evil and Dark One is near,
On an errand of wrath, with his phantoms of fear,

And he knows that the aim of his rifle is vain—
That the spectres of Evil may never be slain!

He knows that the Powwah has cunning and skill,
To call up the Spirit of Darkness at will—
To waken the dead in their wilderness-graves,
And summon the demons of forest and waves.

And he layeth the weapons of battle aside,
And forgetteh the strength of his natural pride,
And he kneels with the priest by his garrisoned door,
That the spectres of Evil may haunt him no more!

THE POWWAW.

THE promontory, called Stratford Point, which stretches into Long Island Sound at the mouth of the Housatonic, is famous as the place of Indian Pow-waws, those strange ceremonies of the Red men, which, if we may believe the account of the early settlers of New-England, were more wild and terrible than those of the ancient Eleusis.

In 1690 the Indians convened in great numbers to hold their annual Powwaw. It lasted several days. The Indians were quiet during the day, but at midnight they gathered together on the sea-shore, and with yells and dancing and frightful gestures, alarmed the white inhabitants for miles around them. The frightful ceremony usually lasted two hours—during which time the good people of Stratford affirmed that they saw demons all on fire, rushing out of the sea, and seizing upon some of the Indians, at which the others seemed highly rejoiced, and the horrible Pow-waw was suspended for the night. In the morning, it is said, that the bones and limbs of the unfortunate Indians who had been sacrificed to Hobamocko, were

8

found scattered along the sea-shore, dreadfully burned, and smelling strongly of brimstone.

In this time of trial for the good puritans of Stratford, it was suggested that the clergymen of the neighborhood should be invited to assemble together and consult for the general safety. They accordingly came together, with divers other goodly persons, and endeavored, by prayer and fasting to lay the infernal Powwaw.

But the evil spirits proved refractory. The Powwaw went on with the most provoking perseverence. The strange fiery figures leaped out of the Sound, as usual, to seize their nightly victims—the same horrible shrieks still rang on the ears of the White men. It was in very deed a fearful time. The old gossips of the neighborhood gathered together every evening around some large, old-fashioned fire-place, where, with ghastly countenances whitening in the dim firelight, the marvellous legends which had been accumulating for more than half a century in the wild woods of the new country, were related, one after another, with hushed voices and tremulous gestures. The mysteries of the Indian worship—the frightful ceremonies of the Powwaw—the incantations and sorceries of the prophets of the wilderness, and their revolting sacrifices to the Evil Being, were all made subjects of these nocturnal gatherings. And even among the other sex the feeling of terror predominated.

> " Old men and beldames in the street
> Did prophesy upon it dangerously,
> And he that spake did gripe the hearer's wrist,
> Whilst he that heard, made fearful action
> With wrinkled brows, and nods and rolling eyes. '

At length a general meeting of the inhabitants was called for the purpose of devising some method of exorcism, potent enough to overcome the strength of the Enemy, and thereby put an end to the infernal orgies of his worshippers. At this meeting, as a last resort, it was proposed to send immediately to a clergyman of New-York of the name of Vicey—a man famous for skill in exorcism, and for his knowledge of the doings of Satan in witchcraft and astrology. The proposal, at first, met with some opposition, inasmuch as he aforesaid Vicey was an Episcopal clergyman, and an enemy to the true vine which had been watered by the tears of the Pilgrims. But the necessity of the case effectually silenced every scruple, and a messenger was forthwith dispatched to invite the New-York clergyman to exercise those powers of exorcism upon an Indian Powwaw, which had been hitherto employed in laying the perturbed ghosts of corpulent Dutchmen, and in driving evil spirits from some goodwife's dairy, or her husband's cabbage-grounds.

The reverend gentleman obeyed with the readiness becoming the urgency of the occasion, the invitation of the good people of Stratford. Fortifying himself with a huge Polyglot bible, and a venerable and well-thumbed prayer-book, he made his appearance on the place of the Powwaw, much to the gratification of the Christians who had so long been annoyed by its unholy revels.

It was a night of November—one of those dark, lowering nights, which are peculiar to the season. There was no rain, but the clouds hung thickly and gloomily around ; while a few grey scuds whirled rapidly over their black masses, like light squadrons hovering along the dark verge of approaching battle. The wind was abroad, shaking the naked boughs of the forest, at gusty and unequal intervals, with formidable power. It was in truth, such an evening as one might readily suppose would be chosen for the revelling of demons and unholy spirits.

> "That night a chield might understand
> The De'il had business on his hand."

On this night, at half past eleven o'clock, a procession was formed from the house of the minister, near the Point, composed of clergymen, deacons, and other

good men and devout. Slowly and cautiously it passed towards the scene of the Powwaw. The torches
and lanthorns of the party cast but a feeble light upon
the rugged pathway, while beyond the circle of that
light, the thick darkness hung above and around, like
a material wall.

The party soon reached a little eminence, which
overlooked the place of the Powwaw. All was still
in every direction—and no living object was visible,
save where along the sea-shore, a few gaunt and half
naked forms, glided like spectres before several new-
ly-lighted fires, which blazed redly into the murky
darkness.

"These are the fires of sacrifice," said one of the
party, in a hushed tone, to the Episcopalian priest.
"They are about to make an offering of one of their
number to the Evil Spirit!"

Even as he spoke, a yell, loud and shrill and horrible burst on the ears of the party; and the broad
space beneath was instantaneously peopled with the
dimly seen forms of the savages. Strange lights went
dancing through the air, and shone over the agitated
waters, and grim figures, apparently circled with
flames, leaped out from the beach as if from the bosom of the sea. And wilder and more terrible the
fierce yells were repeated—

"As if the very fiends that fell
Had pealed the banner cry of Hell!"

"In the strength of the Lord let us go on!" said the Episcopalian. And the procession passed down the hill towards the shouting savages, with a slow and solemn tread.

"Aroint ye, evil spirits!" shouted the priest—"aroint ye, in the name of the Lord!"

The savages turned suddenly towards the solemn procession. In its front stood the tall form of the reverend exorciser—his grey locks blowing in the wind, with the glare of a dozen torches flashing around him—and his arms tossing aloft, as with a loud and strong voice he shouted forth his exorcism.

"Hobamocko! Hobamocko!" shrieked the Indians, at this startling interruption of their ceremonies. It came upon them wildly, spectre-like, and as a vision from another world—a visitation of some offended Power. With one voice, they sent up the cry of "Hobamocko!" and fled precipitately in all directions. The great Powwaw was broken up—and never afterwards was the neighborhood troubled with similar visitations.

The fame of the New-York clergyman was completely established—and the good puritans of Stratford learned to think more favorably of the peculiar

doctrines of his faith, after such a convincing display
of his power over the evil spirits of the Powwaw.—
Even the most rigid admitted the fact of his skill in
the difficult matters of exorcism, especially, when they
remembered that even as Moses did of old—the Pagan magicians did with their enchantments.

NOTE.—The substance of the foregoing sketch may be found in a curious
book, written by " a gentleman of Connecticut," and first published in 1731,
in London. The book contains, with many and manifold absurdities, a val-
uable collection of amusing anecdotes and historical facts.

THE SPECTRE SHIP.

[The Legend of the Spectre Ship of Salem is still preserved among some of the old descendants of the puritans. A particular description of the preternatural visitation is given in "Magnalia Christi Americana." The story is that a ship, which left Salem sometime during the 17th century for "old England," contained, among other passengers, a young man of a strange and wild appearance, and a girl, still younger, and of surpassing beauty. She was deadly pale, and trembled, even while she leaned on the arm of her companion. No one knew them—they spoke not—they paid no regard to anything around them. This excited the alarm of some of the credulous people of the place, who supposed them to be demons: and who, in consequence, endeavored to dissuade their friends from entering the ship—notwithstanding which, a goodly number went on board. The remainder of the story is told in the following lines.]

"THE morning light is breaking forth
    All over the dark blue sea—
And the waves are changed—they are rich with gold
    As the morning waves should be,
And the rising winds are wandering out
    On their seaward pinions free.

The bark is ready—the sails are set,
    And the boat rocks on the shore—
Say why do the passengers linger yet?—
    Is not the farewell o'er?
Do those who enter that gallant ship
    Go forth to return no more?"

A wailing rose by the water-side,
   A young, fair girl was there—
With a face as pale as the face of **Death**
   When its coffin-lid is bare ;—
And an eye as strangely beautiful
   As a star in the upper air.

She leaned on a youthful stranger's arm,
   A tall and silent one—
Who stood in the very midst of the **crowd,**
   Yet uttered a word to none ;
He gazed on the sea and the waiting **ship**—
   But he gazed on them alone !

The fair girl leaned on the stranger's **arm,**
   And she wept as one in fear,
But he heeded not the plaintive **moan**
   And the dropping of the tear ;—
His eye was fixed on the stirring **sea,**
   Cold, darkly and severe !

The boat was filled—the shore was left—
   The farewell word was said—
But the vast crowd lingered still behind
   With an over-powering dread ;

They feared that stranger and his bride,
   So pale and like the dead.

And many said that an evil pair
   Among their friends had gone,—
A demon with his human prey,
   From the quiet grave-yard drawn ;
And a prayer was heard that the innocent
   Might escape the Evil One.

Away—the good ship sped away,
   Out on the broad high seas—
The sun upon her path before—
   Behind, the steady breeze—
And there was naught in sea or sky
   Of fearful auguries.

The day passed on—the sunlight fell
   All slantwise from the west,
And then the heavy clouds of storm
   Sat on the ocean's breast ;
And every swelling billow mourn'd
   Like a living thing distressed.

The sun went down among the clouds,
   Tinging with sudden gold,

The pall-like shadow of the storm,
  On every mighty fold—
And then the lightning's eye look'd forth,
  And the red thunder rolled.

The storm came down upon the sea,
  In its surpassing dread,
Rousing the white and broken surge
  Above its rocky bed,
As if the deep was stirred beneath
  A giant's viewless tread.

All night the hurricane went on,
  And all along the shore,
The smothered cry of shipwreck'd men
  Blent with the ocean's roar;—
The grey-haired man had scarcely known
  So wild a night before.

Morn rose upon a tossing sea,
  The tempest's work was done,
And freely over land and wave,
  Shone out the blessed sun—
But where was she—that merchant-bark—
  Where had the good ship gone!

Men gathered on the shore to watch
   The billow's heavy swell,
Hoping, yet fearing much, some frail
   Memorial might tell
The fate of that disastrous ship,—
   Of friends they loved so well.

None came—the billows smoothed away—
   And all was strangely calm,
As if the very sea had felt
   A necromancer's charm ;
And not a trace was left behind,
   Of violence and harm.

The twilight came with sky of gold—
   And curtaining of night—
And then a sudden cry rang out,
   "A ship—*the* ship in sight !"
And lo !—tall masts grew visible
   Within the fading light.

Near and more near the ship came on,
   With all her broad sails spread—
The night grew thick, but a phantom light
   Around her path was shed,

And the gazers shuddered as on she came,
　For against the wind she sped.

They saw by the dim and baleful glare
　Around that voyager thrown,
The upright forms of the well known crew,
　As pale and fixed as stone—
And they called to them, but no sound came back,
　Save the echoed cry alone.

The fearful stranger-youth was there,
　And clasped in his embrace,
The pale and passing sorrowful
　Gazed wildly in his face ;—
Like one who had been wakened from
　The silent burial-place.

A shudder ran along the crowd—
　And a holy man knelt there,
On the wet sea-sand, and offered up
　A faint and trembling prayer,
That God would shield his people from
　The Spirits of the air !

And lo !—the vision passed away—
　The Spectre Ship—the crew—

The stranger and his pallid bride,
   Departed from their view ;
And nought was left upon the waves
   Beneath the arching blue.

It passed away—that vision strange—
   Forever from their sight,—
Yet, long shall Naumkeag's annals tell
   The story of that night—
The phantom-bark—the ghostly crew—
   The pale, encircling light.

THE HUMAN SACRIFICE.

"O'er Moodus river a light has glanced—
On Moodus hills it shone."

J. G. C. Brainard.

THE township of East-Haddam was originally the possession of a ferocious tribe of Indians, distinguished by the name of Matchit-Moodus—a powerful and warlike tribe, essentially distinct from their neighbors, and remarkable for their idolatries and pagan rites. It is a general remark that the aborigines of New-England paid little reverence to religious rites of any kind whatever. They indeed spoke of the Great Spirit with awe, when his loud thunder was bursting above them—but they knelt not in worship at the rising and the going down of the sun—they built up no rude altars, and made no important sacrifices to the unknown Deity—Yet, with the tribe of Matchit-Moodus, the rites of the Pawwaw and the strange worship of good and bad spirits were observed and reverenced, as religiously as the Mahometan ablutions —the pagoda-worship of the Brahmin—or the oblations to the fiery altars of the Gheber.

The first settlement of the white men upon the ter-

ritory of the Indians of Matchit-Moodus occasioned
no inconsiderable alarm to the jealous chiefs of the
tribe. Indeed, at the period to which this story relates,
in all parts of New-England the white men were
viewed with distrust, even in their feeblest settlements.

In many places hostilities were carried on with
fierceness on both sides ; and every where the impla-
cable hate of the Red-man was brooding like a thunder-cloud over the encroaching advance of the English. And ever where a temporary forbearance was
manifested on the part of the savages, it proved too
often, like the couch of the panther or the coil of the
roused rattlesnake, but the preparation for a sudden
and deadly blow

It was a day of Autumn in 1670. The first heavy
frosts had fallen upon the beautiful forests which then
overhung the whole extent of the majestic Connecticut,
and a wild change had followed their blighting visitation. The vast and unshorn foliage, whose trunks
had as yet bowed only to the presence of the storm or
the weight of accumulated centuries, was colored
with dyes deeper and richer than any which Claude
or Poussin ever mingled—varied and magnificent, as
if the rainbow of a summer shower had fallen upon it
and blended with its green luxuriance.

At the foot of one of those ragged hills which frown over the quiet waters of the Connecticut on its western side, a large band of Indian warriors, painted and adorned for the performance of their dark rites of worship, were assembled. In their midst, a young and interesting female was seated, whose pale, fair countenance and plain and modest garb, distinguished her as the daughter of one of the white settlers. She was young—apparently not more than fifteen years of age—and, though agitated at times with terror, her features were regular and beautiful, and her eye, although filled with tears, shone brightly through the profusion of rich, light curls, which partially over-shadowed her fine countenance.

The Indians drew themselves into a circle around her, and knelt down, smiting slowly and solemnly on the ground, and humming between their closed teeth a wild and unnatural air. An old, fierce-looking chief now came forward, into the centre of the ring, by the side of the white prisoner. Placing himself in the attitude of a priest at the sacrifice, he addressed his red brethren. The strange hum died away, and every one leaned eagerly forward as he spoke :

"Brothers ! The little white snake came to the den of the big snake of the rocks. And the big snake bade him lie down with him and eat of his

9*

food, for the little snake was hungry and very cold. And the little white snake eat of the food and lay by the side of the big snake. But when the big snake was asleep the white snake sucked his blood, and when the big snake awoke he was very weak, and the little white snake had grown big as himself.

" Brothers !—The white man is the little snake and the red man is the big snake. The white snake has been sucking his blood. He has grown very big.

" Brothers !—The wicked spirits are with the white men. Their powwahs are stronger than ours, and the bad spirits obey them. The red man cannot call them.

" Brothers !—Let us make an offering to the bad spirits, that they may love us and obey us. The daughter of the white man is before us. Let us make the dark spirits glad. They will smell the blood. Hobamocko loves the blood of the pale-face."

A hum of assent passed round the kneeling circle. The chief muttered some strange words of invocation, and drawing his long knife from his belt, he grasped the fair hair of his victim.

The unfortunate girl had resigned herself to her seemingly inevitable fate—and, falling on her knees, she clasped her hands over her eyes, and murmured a few broken and inarticulate words of prayer.

"She is talking with the Englishman's God," said the Powwah.

At that moment, a low, rumbling sound burst from the bosom of the hill. The dwarfish trees and stinted bushes trembled around, as if an imprisoned earthquake were shaking off its rocky chains and struggling upward. The Indians fell on their faces to the ground.

"It is the voice of the Great Spirit!" said the Powwah, in the thick and husky tones of terror, as he unloosed his grasp upon the hair of his prisoner.

Again the strange sound was heard—an inward rumbling—a shaking of the hill, as if some gigantic creature of life were bursting through its prison walls of everlasting rock.

The Powwah uttered a yell of terror, and darted from the spot, with the arrow-like speed peculiar to his race. The yell was repeated by his companions, who fled in every direction, like deer before the hunters.

The fair-haired daughter of the white man returned to tell the miraculous story of her escape from the grim worshippers of Moodus. The Indians ever after avoided the mysterious hill, as the chosen dwelling-place of the Great Spirit of the Yengeese.

NOTE.—The early settlers of the valley of the Connecticut were under the firm belief that the Indians of Matchit-Moodus, offered human sacrifices to their evil spirit, or Hobamocko. The legend of the "*Moodus noises*" is one of the most singular which has ever reached our knowledge. It is said that these noises, which growled occasionally from a hill or mountain in East Haddam, created much alarm among the early settlers of the country. There is a story prevalent in the neighborhood that a man from England, a kind of astrologer or necromancer, undertook to rid the place of the troublesome noises. He told them that the sound proceeded from a carbuncle—a precious gem, *growing in the bowels of the rock*. He hired an old blacksmith's shop, and worked for some time with closed doors, and at night. All at once the necromancer departed, and the strange noises ceased. It was supposed he had found the precious gem, and had fled with it to his native land. The following is an extract from a poem written upon this singular legend by the lamented Brainard:

"Now upward goes that gray old man,
　With mattock, bar and spade—
The summit is gain'd, and the toil began,
And deep by the rock where the wild lights ran,
　The magic trench is made."

"Then upward stream'd the brilliant's light,
　It stream'd o'er crag and stone :—
Dim look'd the stars, and the moon, that night;
But when morning came in her glory bright,
　The man and the jewel were gone.

"But wo to the bark in which he flew
　From Moodus' rocky shore;
Wo to the Captain, and wo to the crew,
That ever the breath of life they drew,
　When that dreadful freight they bore.

"Where is that crew and vessel now?
　Tell me their state who can?
The wild waves dash o'er their sinking bow—
Down, down to the fathomless depths the go,
　To sleep with a sinful man.

"The carbuncle lies in the deep, deep sea,
   Beneath the mighty wave;
But the light shines upward so gloriously,
That the sailor looks pale, and forgets his glee,
   When he crosses the wizard's grave.' '

THE INDIAN'S TALE.

NOTE.—It was generally believed, by the first settlers of New-England, that a mortal pestilence had, a short time previous to their arrival, in a great measure depopulated some of the finest portions of the country on the seaboard. The Indians themselves corroborated this opinion, and gave the English a terrific description of the ravages of the unseen Destroyer.

THE War-God did not wake to strife,
　The strong men of our forest-land,
No red hand grasped the battle-knife
　At Areouski's high command :—
We held no war-dance by the dim
　And red light of the creeping flame ;
Nor warrior-yell, nor battle-hymn
　Upon the midnight breezes came.

There was no portent in the sky,
　No shadow on the round, bright sun,
With light and mirth and melody,
　The long, fair summer days came on ;
We were a happy people then,
　Rejoicing in our hunter-mood ;
No foot-prints of the pale-faced men
　Had marred our forest-solitude.

The land was ours—this glorious land—
  With all its wealth of wood and streams—
Our warriors strong of heart and hand—
  Our daughters beautiful as dreams.
When wearied at the thirsty noon,
  We knelt us where the spring gushed up
To taste our Father's blessed boon—
  Unlike the white-man's poison cup.

There came unto my father's hut,
  A wan, weak creature of distress;
The red man's door is never shut
  Against the lone and shelterless;
And when he knelt before his feet,
  My father led the stranger in—
He gave him of his hunter-meat—
  Alas! it was a deadly sin!

The stranger's voice was not like ours—
  His face at first was sadly pale,
Anon 'twas like the yellow flowers,
  Which tremble in the meadow-gale—
And when he laid him down to die—
  And murmured of his father-land,
My mother wiped his tearful eye,
  My father held his burning hand!

He died at last—the funeral yell
   Rang upward from his burial sod,
And the old Powwah knelt to tell
   The tidings to the white man's God !
The next day came—my father's brow
   Grew heavy with a fearful pain,
He did not take his hunting-bow—
   He never sought the woods again !

He died even as the white-man died—-
   My mother, she was smitten too,
My sisters vanished from my side,
   Like diamonds from the sun-lit dew.
And then we heard the Powwahs say—
   That God had sent his angel forth,
To sweep our ancient tribes away—
   And poison and unpeople Earth.

And it was so—-from day to day
   The Spirit of the Plague went on—
And those at morning blithe and gay,
   Were dying at the set of sun.
They died—our free, bold hunters died—-
   The living might not give them graves—
Save when along the water-side
   They cast them to the hurrying waves.

The carrion crow—the ravenous beast,
    Turned loathing from the ghastly dead ;
Well might they shun the funeral feast
    By that destroying angel spread !
One after one, the red-men fell,
    Our gallant war-tribe passed away—
And I alone am left to tell
    The story of its swift decay.

Alone—alone—a withered leaf,
    Yet clinging to its naked bough ;
The pale race scorn the aged chief,
    And I will join my fathers now.
The Spirits of my people bend
    At midnight from the solemn West,
To me their kindly arms extend—
    To call me to their home of rest !

10

A NIGHT AMONG THE WOLVES.

—————" The gaunt wolf,
Scenting the place of slaughter with his long
And most offensive howl, did ask for blood!"

THE wolf—the gaunt and ferocious wolf! How
many tales of wild horror are associated with its
name! Tales of the deserted battle-field—where the
wolf and the vulture feast together—a horrible and
obscene banquet, realizing the fearful description of
the Seige of Corinth, when—

—————" On the edge of a gulf
There sat a raven flapping a wolf,"

amidst the cold and stiffening corses of the fallen;—
or of the wild Scandinavian forests, where the pea-
sant sinks down, exhausted amidst the drifts of winter,
and the wild wolf-howl sounds fearfully in his deafen-
ing ear, and lean forms and evil eyes gather closer
and closer around him, as if impatient for the death of
the doomed victim.

The early settlers of New-England were, not unfrequently, greatly incommoded by the numbers and fe-
rocity of the wolves which prowled around their rude

settlements. The hunter easily overpowered them, and with one discharge of his musket, scattered them from about his dwelling. They fled, even from the timid child, in the broad glare of day—but in the thick and solitary night, far away from the dwellings of men, they were terrible, from their fiendish and ferocious appetite for blood.

I have heard a fearful story of the wolf, from the lips of some of the old settlers of Vermont. Perhaps it may be best told in the language of one of the witnesses of the scene.

" 'Twas a night of January, in the year 17—. We had been to a fine quilting frolic, about two miles from our little settlement of four or five log-houses. 'Twas rather late—about 12 o'clock, I should guess—when the party broke up. There was no moon—and a dull, grey shadow or haze hung all around the horizon, while overhead a few pale and sickly looking stars gave us their dull light as if they shone through a dingy curtain. There were six of us in company— Harry Mason and myself and four as pretty girls as ever grew up this side of the Green Mountains. There were my two sisters and Harry's sister and his sweetheart, the daughter of our next door neighbor. She was a right down handsome girl—that Caroline Allen. I never saw her equal, 'though I am no

stranger to pretty faces. She was so pleasant and
kind of heart—so gentle and sweet-spoken, and so in-
telligent besides, that every body loved her. She
had an eye as blue as the hill-violet, and her lips were
like a red rose-leaf in June. No wonder that Harry
Mason loved her—boy though he was—for we had
neither of us seen our seventeenth summer.

   " Our path lay through a thick forest of oak, with
here and there a tall pine raising its dark, full shadow
against the sky, with an outline rendered indistinct by
the thick darkness. The snow was deep—deeper a
great deal than it ever falls of late years—but the sur-
face was frozen strongly enough to bear our weight,
and we hurried on over the white pathway with rapid
steps. We had not proceeded far, before a low, long
howl came to our ears. We all knew it in a moment :
and I could feel a shudder thrilling the arms that were
folded close to my own, as a sudden cry burst from
the lips of all of us—" The wolves—the wolves!"

   " Did you ever see a wild wolf—not one of your
caged, broken down show-animals, which are exhibit-
ed for sixpence a sight—children half price—but a
fierce, half-starved ranger of the wintry forest—howling and hurrying over the barren snow, and actually
mad with hunger ? There is no one of God's creatures which has such a frightful, fiendish look, as this

animal. It has the form as well as the spirit of a demon.

"Another, and another howl—and then we could hear distinctly the quick patter of feet behind us. We all turned right about, and looked in the direction of the sound.

"The devils are after us," said Mason, pointing to a line of dark, gliding bodies. And so in fact they were—a whole troop of them--howling like so many Indians in a Powwaw. We had no weapons of any kind ; and we knew enough of the nature of the vile creatures who followed us to feel that it would be useless for us to contend without them. There was not a moment to lose—the savage beasts were close upon us. To attempt flight would have been a hopeless affair. There was but one chance of escape, and we instantly seized upon it.

"To the tree—let us climb this tree!" I cried, springing forward towards a low-boughed and gnarled oak, which I saw at a glance might be easily climbed into.

"Harry Mason sprang lightly into the tree, and aided in placing the terrified girls in a place of comparative security among the thick boughs. I was the last on the ground, and the whole troop were yelling at my heels before I reached the rest of the company.

10*

There was one moment of hard breathing and wild
exclamations among us, and then a feeling of calm
thankfulness for our escape.   The night was cold—
and we soon began to shiver and shake, like so many
sailors on the top-mast of an Iceland whaler.   But
there were no murmurs—no complaining among us—
for we could distinctly see the gaunt, attenuated bodies of the wolves beneath us, and every now and
then we could see great, glowing eyes, staring up into
the tree where we were seated.   And then their yells
—they were loud and long and devilish !

"I know not how long we had remained in this
situation, for we had no means of ascertaining the
time—when I heard a limb of the tree cracking, as if
breaking down beneath the weight of some of us ;
and a moment after a shriek went through my ears
like the piercing of a knife.   A light form went plun-
ging down through the naked branches, and fell with
a dull and heavy sound upon the stiff snow.

" *Oh God ! I am gone !*"

" It was the voice of Caroline Allen. The poor
girl never spoke again !   There was a horrible dizzi-
ness and confusion in my brain, and I spoke not—
and I stirred not—for the whole was at that time like
an ugly, unreal dream.   I only remember that there
were cries and shudderings around me—perhaps I

joined with them—and that there were smothered
groans and dreadful howls underneath. It was all
over in a moment. Poor Caroline! She was literally
eaten alive. The wolves had a frightful feast, and
they became raving mad with the taste of blood.

" When I came fully to myself—when the horrible
dream went off—and it lasted but a moment—I struggled to shake off the arms of my sisters, which were
clinging around me, and could I have cleared myself
I should have jumped down among the raging animals.
But when a second thought came over me, I knew
that any attempt at rescue would be useless. As for
poor Mason, he was wild with horror. He had tried
to follow Caroline when she fell—but he could not
shake off the grasp of his terrified sister. His youth,
and weak constitution and frame, were unable to
withstand the dreadful trial; and he stood close by
my side, with his hands firmly clenched and his teeth
set closely, gazing down upon the dark, wrangling
creatures below, with the fixed stare of a maniac. It
was indeed a terrible scene. Around us was the
thick, cold night—and below, the ravenous wild
beasts were lapping their bloody jaws, and howling
for another victim.

" The morning broke at last; and our frightful enemies fled at the first advance of day-light, like so

many cowardly murderers. We waited until the sun had risen before we ventured to crawl down from our resting-place. We were chilled through—every limb was numb with cold and terror—and poor Mason was delirious, and raved wildly about the dreadful things he had witnessed. There were bloody stains all around the tree; and two or three long locks of dark hair were trampled into the snow.

"We had gone but a little distance when we were met by our friends from the settlement, who had become alarmed at our absence. They were shocked at our wild and frightful appearance; and my brothers have oftentimes told me that at first view we all seemed like so many crazed and brain-stricken creatures. They assisted us to reach our homes; but Harry Mason never recovered fully from the dreadful trial. He neglected his business, his studies and his friends, and would sit alone for hours together, ever and anon muttering to himself about that horrible night. He fell to drinking soon after, and died, a miserable drunkard, before age had whitened a hair of his head.

"For my own part, I confess I have never entirely overcome the terrors of the melancholy circumstance which I have endeavored to describe. The thought of it has haunted me like my own shadow. And even now, the whole scene comes at times freshly before me in my dreams, and I start up with something of the same feeling of terror, as when, more than half a century ago, I passed A NIGHT AMONG THE WOLVES."

NOTE.—Perhaps the foregoing may be deemed improbable. It is however an oral tradition, which is as well authenticated as anything of the kind may well be. It is one of a series of strange legends of encounters with the wild beasts of a new country which have descended to us from our hardy forefathers, and which are still preserved in the memories of their children.

THE WHITE MOUNTAINS.

[The Indians supposed the White Mountains to be the residence of certain powerful Spirits, and consequently never ventured to ascend them. This curious tradition is preserved in Josselyn's Rarities of New-England. The following is supposed to be the address of an Indian of the present day to the mountain which his fathers reverenced.]

GREY searcher of the upper air!
  There's sunshine on thy ancient walls—
A crown upon thy forehead bare—
  A flashing on thy water-falls!—
A rainbow glory in the cloud,
Upon thine awful summit bowed,
  Dim relic of the recent storm!—
And music, from the leafy shroud
Which wraps in green thy giant form,
Mellowed and softened from above,
  Steals down upon the listening ear,
Sweet as the maiden's dream of love,
  With soft tones melting on her ear.

The time has been, grey mountain, when
  Thy shadows veiled the red-man's home;
And over crag and serpent-den,
And wild gorge, where the steps of men

In chase or battle might not come,
The mountain-eagle bore on high
  The emblem of the free of soul;
And midway in the fearful sky
Sent back the Indian's battle-cry,
  Or answered to the thunder's roll.

The wigwam fires have all burned out—
  The moccasin hath left no track—
Nor wolf nor wild-deer roam about
  The Saco or the Merrimack;
And thou that liftest up on high
Thine awful barriers to the sky,
  Art not the haunted mount of old,
When on each crag of blasted stone
Some mountain-spirit found a throne,
  And shrieked from out the thick cloud-fold—
And answered to the Thunderer's cry
When rolled the car of tempest by;
And jutting rock and riven branch
Went down before the avalanche.

The Father of our people then,
  Upon thine awful summit trod,
And the red dwellers of the glen
  Bowed down before the Indian's God.

There, when His shadow veiled the sky,
　　The Thunderer's voice was long and loud,
And the red flashes of His eye
　　Were pictured on the o'erhanging cloud

That Spirit moveth there no more—
　　The dwellers of the hills have gone—
The sacred groves are trampled o'er,
　　And foot-prints mar the altar-stone.
The white man climbs thy tallest rock,
　　And hangs him from the mossy steep,
Where, trembling to the cloud-fire's shock,
Thy ancient prison-walls unlock,
And captive waters leap to light,
And dancing down from height to height,
　　Pass onward to the far-off deep.

Oh sacred to the Indian seer,
　　Grey altar of the days of old !
Still are thy rugged features dear,
As when unto my infant ear
　　The legends of the past were told.
Tales of the downward sweeping flood,
When bowed like reeds thy ancient wood,—
　　Of armed hand and spectral form,
Of giants in their misty shroud,

And voices calling long and loud,
  In the drear pauses of the storm !
Farewell !—The red man's face is turned
  Towards another hunting ground ;
For where the council-fire has burned,
  And o'er the sleeping warrior's mound
Another fire is kindled now—
Its light is on the white man's brow !
  The hunter-race have passed away—
Ay, vanished like the morning mist,
Or dew-drops by the sunshine kissed,—
  And wherefore should the red man stay ?

11

THE BLACK FOX.

[There is a strange legend relative to the "Black Fox of Salmon River" Connecticut, which has been versified below. Brainard alludes to it in one of his finest poems:]

"And there the Black Fox roved and howled and shook
His thick tail to the hunters."

IT was a cold and cruel night,
  Some fourscore years ago—
The clouds across the winter sky
  Were scudding to and fro—
The air above was cold and keen,
  The earth was white below.

Around an ancient fire-place,
  A happy household drew;
The husband and his own good wife
  And children not a few;
And bent above the spinning-wheel
  The aged grandame too.

The fire-light reddened all the room,
  It rose so high and strong;
And mirth was in each pleasant eye

Within that household throng—
And while the grandame turned her wheel
    The good man hummed a song.

At length spoke up a fair-haired girl,
    Some seven summers old,
"Now, grandame, tell the tale again
    Which yesterday you told;
About the Black Fox and the men
    Who followed him so bold."

"Yes, tell it," said a dark-eyed boy,
    And "tell it," said his brother—
"Just tell the story of the Fox,
    We will not ask another;"
And all the children gathered close
    Around their old grandmother.

Then lightly in her withered hands
    The grandame turned her reel,
And when the thread was wound away
    She set aside her wheel,
And smiled with that peculiar joy
    The old and happy feel.

"'Tis more than sixty years ago
    Since first the Fox was seen—

'Twas in the winter of the year,
  When not a leaf was green,
Save where the dark, old hemlock stood
  The naked oaks between.

My father saw the creature first,
  One bitter winter's day—
It passed so near that he could see
  Its fiery eye-balls play,
And well he knew an evil thing
  And foul had crossed his way.

A hunter like my father then,
  We never more shall see—
The mountain-cat was not more swift
  Of eye and foot than he:
His aim was fatal in the air
  And on the tallest tree.

Yet close beneath his ready aim
  The Black Fox hurried on,
And when the forest-echoes mocked
  The sharp voice of his gun—
The creature gave a frightful yell,
  Long, loud, but only one.

And there was something horrible
    And fiendish in that yell;
Our good old parson heard it once,
    And I have heard him tell
That it might well be likened to
    A fearful cry from hell.

Day after day that Fox was seen,
    He prowled our forests through,
Still gliding wild and spectre-like
    Before the hunter's view;
And howling louder than the storm
    When savagely it blew.

The Indians, when upon the wind
    That howl rose long and clear,
Shook their wild heads mysteriously
    And muttered, as in fear;
Or veiled their eyes, as if they knew
    An evil thing was near.

They said it was a Fox accurst
    By Hobomocko's will,
That it was once a mighty chief
    Whom battle might not kill,
                11*

But who, for some unspoken crime,
   Was doomed to wander still.

That every year, when all the hills
   Were white with winter snow,
And the tide of Salmon River ran
   The gathering ice below ;
His howl was heard and his form was seen
   Still hurrying to and fro.

At length two gallant hunter-youths,
   The boast and pride of all—
The gayest in the hour of mirth,
   The first at danger's call,
Our playmates at the village-school,
   Our partners at the ball—

Went forth to hunt the Sable Fox
   Beside that haunted stream,
Where it so long had glided like
   The creature of a dream—
Or like unearthly forms that dance
   Under the cold moon-beam !

They went away one winter day,
   When all the air was white,
And thick and hazed with falling snow,

And blinding to the sight;
They bade us never fear for them—
    They would return by night.

The night fell thick and darkly down,
    And still the storm blew on;
And yet the hunters came not back,
    Their task was yet undone;
Nor came they with their words of cheer,
    Even with the morrow's sun.

And then our old men shook their heads,
    And the red Indians told
Their tales of evil sorcery,
    Until our blood ran cold,—
The stories of their Powwah seers,
    And withered hags of old.

They told us that our hunters
    Would never more return—
That they would hunt for evermore
    Through tangled swamp and fern,
And that their last and dismal fate
    No mortal ear might learn.

And days and weeks passed slowly on,
    And yet they came not back,

Nor ever more, by stream or hill,
  Was seen that form of black—
Alas! for those who hunted still
  Within its fearful track !

But when the winter passed away,
  And early flowers began
To bloom along the sunned hill-side,
  And where the waters ran,
There came unto my father's door
  A melancholy man.

His form had not the sign of years,
  And yet his locks were white,
And in his deep and restless eye
  There was a fearful light,
And from its glance we turned away,
  As from an adder's sight.

We placed our food before that man,
  So haggard and so wild,—
He thrust it from his lips as he
  Had been a fretful child ;
And when we spoke with words of cheer,
  Most bitterly he smiled.

He smiled, and then a gush of tears,
  And then a fierce, wild look ;
And then he murmured of the Fox
  Which haunted Salmon Brook,
Until his hearers every one
  With nameless terror shook.

He turned away with a frightful cry,
  And hurried madly on,
As if the dark and spectral thing
  Before his path had gone—
We called him back, but he heeded not
  The kind and warning tone.

He came not back to us again,
  But the Indian hunters said
That far, where the howling wilderness
  Its leafy tribute shed,
They found our missing hunters
  Naked and cold and dead.

Their grave they made beneath the shade
  Of the old and solemn wood,
Where oaks, by Time alone hewn down,
  For centuries had stood—

And left them without shroud or prayer
In the dark solitude.

The Indians always shun that grave—
The wild deer treads not there—
The green grass is not trampled down
By catamount or bear,—
The soaring wild-bird turns away,
Even in the upper air.

For people say that every year,
When winter snows are spread
All over the face of the frozen earth,
And the forest leaves are shed,
The Spectre-Fox comes forth and howls
Above the hunters' bed."

THE MOTHER'S REVENGE.

WOMAN's attributes are generally considered of a milder and purer character than those of man. The virtues of meek affection, of fervent piety, of winning sympathy and of that " charity which forgiveth often," are more peculiarly her own. Her sphere of action is generally limited to the endearments of home—the quiet communion with her friends, and the angelic exercise of the kindly charities of existence. Yet, there have been astonishing manifestations of female fortitude and power in the ruder and sterner trials of humanity ; manifestations of a courage rising almost to sublimity; the revelation of all those dark and terrible passions, which madden and distract the heart of manhood.

The perils which surrounded the earliest settlers of New-England were of the most terrible character. None but such a people as were our forefathers could have successfully sustained them. In the dangers and the hardihood of that perilous period, woman herself shared largely. It was not unfrequently her task to garrison the dwelling of her absent husband, and hold

at bay the fierce savages in their hunt for blood.
Many have left behind them a record of their suffer-
ings and trials in the great wilderness, when in the
bondage of the heathen, which are full of wonderful
and romantic incidents, related however without os-
tentation, plainly and simply, as if the authors felt
assured that they had only performed the task which
Providence had set before them, and for which they
could ask no tribute of admiration.

In 1698 the Indians made an attack upon the English settlement at Haverhill—now a beautiful village
on the left bank of the Merrimack.   They surrounded
the house of one Duston, which was a little removed
from the main body of the settlement.   The wife of
Duston was at that time in bed with an infant child in
her arms.   Seven young children were around her.
On the first alarm Duston bade his children fly towards the Garrison-house, and then turned to save his
wife and infant.   By this time the savages were press-
ing close upon them.   The heroic woman saw the
utter impossibility of her escape—and she bade her
husband fly to succor his children, and leave her to
her fate.   It was a moment of terrible trial for the
husband—he hesitated between his affection and his
duty—but the entreaties of his wife fixed his determination.

He turned away, and followed his children. A part of the Indians pursued him, but he held them at a distance by the frequent discharge of his rifle. The children fled towards the garrison, where their friends waited, with breathless anxiety, to receive them. More than once, during their flight, the savages gained upon them; but a shot from the rifle of Duston, followed, as it was, by the fall of one of their number, effectually checked their progress. The garrison was reached, and Duston and his children, exhausted with fatigue and terror, were literally dragged into its enclosure by their anxious neighbors.

Mrs. Duston, her servant girl and her infant were made prisoners by the Indians, and were compelled to proceed before them in their retreat towards their lurking-place. The charge of her infant necessarily impeded her progress; and the savages could ill brook delay when they knew the avenger of blood was following closely behind them. Finding that the wretched mother was unable to keep pace with her captors, the leader of the band approached her, and wrested the infant from her arms. The savage held it before him for a moment, contemplating, with a smile of grim fierceness the terrors of its mother, and then dashed it from him with all his powerful strength. Its head smote heavily on the trunk of an adjacent

12

tree, and the dried leaves around were sprinkled with brains and blood.

" Go on !" said the Indian.

The wretched mother cast one look upon her dead infant, and another to Heaven, as she obeyed her savage conductor. She has often said, that at this moment, all was darkness and horror—that her very heart seemed to cease beating, and to lie cold and dead in her bosom, and that her limbs moved only as involuntary machinery. But when she gazed around her and saw the unfeeling savages, grinning at her and mocking her, and pointing to the mangled body of her infant with fiendish exultation, a new and terrible feeling came over her. It was the thirst of revenge ; and from that moment her purpose was fixed. There was a thought of death at her heart—an insatiate longing for blood. An instantaneous change had been wrought in her very nature ; the angel had become a demon,—and she followed her captors, with a stern determination to embrace the earliest opportunity for a bloody retribution.

The Indians followed the course of the Merrimack, until they had reached their canoes, a distance of seventy or eighty miles. They paddled to a small island, a little above the upper falls of the river. Here they kindled a fire ; and fatigued by their long marches and sleepless nights, stretched themselves around it, without dreaming of the escape of their captives.

Their sleep was deep—deeper than any which the white man knows,—a sleep from which they were never to awaken. The two captives lay silent, until the hour of midnight; but the bereaved mother did not close her eyes. There was a gnawing of revenge at her heart, which precluded slumber. There was a spirit within her which defied the weakness of the body.

She rose up and walked around the sleepers, in order to test the soundness of their slumber. They stirred not limb or muscle. Placing a hatchet in the hands of her fellow captive, and bidding her stand ready to assist her, she grasped another in her own hands, and smote its ragged edge deeply into the skull of the nearest sleeper. A slight shudder and a feeble groan followed. The savage was dead. She passed on to the next. Blow followed blow, until ten out of twelve, the whole number of the savages, were stiffening in blood. One escaped with a dreadful wound. The last—a small boy—still slept amidst the scene of carnage. Mrs. Duston lifted her dripping hatchet above his head, but hesitated to strike the blow.

"It is a poor boy," she said, mentally, "a poor
child, and perhaps he has a mother!" The thought
of her own children rushed upon her mind, and she
spared him. She was in the act of leaving the bloody
spot, when, suddenly reflecting that the people of her
settlement would not credit her story, unsupported by
any proof save her own assertion, she returned and
deliberately scalped her ten victims. With this fearful evidence of her prowess, she loosed one of the
Indian canoes, and floated down the river to the falls,
from which place she travelled through the wilderness to the residence of her husband.

Such is the simple and unvarnished story of a New-
England woman. The curious historian, who may
hereafter search among the dim records of our " twilight time"—who may gather from the uncertain re-
sponses of tradition, the wonderful history of the past
—will find much, of a similar character, to call forth
by turns, admiration and horror. And the time is
coming, when all these traditions shall be treasured
up as a sacred legacy—when the tale of the Indian inroad and the perils of the hunter—of the sublime
courage and the dark superstitions of our ancestors,
will be listened to with an interest unknown to the
present generation,—and those who are to fill our
places will pause hereafter by the Indian's burial-

place, and on the scite of the old battle-field, or the thrown-down garrison, with a feeling of awe and reverence, as if communing, face to face, with the spirits of that stern race, which has passed away forever.

12*

THE AERIAL OMENS.

[The Aurora Borealis, previous to the "Old French War" and the War of the Revolution, was uncommonly brilliant, and of a strange and mysterious appearance. It was supposed that an army of fiery warriors were seen in the sky, with banners floating, and plumes tossing, and horsemen hurrying to and fro. The superstitions of that period are still fresh in the minds of our oldest inhabitants. The strange changes of the Borealis were considered by many as ominous of approaching war ; and consequently excited no little apprehension. The breaking out of war soon after, completely confirmed this supposition; and many an aged Revolutionist will yet tell of the wonderful Northern Lights, and that he saw the battles of Saratoga and Bennington, pictured distinctly on the sky, long before their actual occurrence.]

A LIGHT is troubling Heaven !—A strange, dull glow
Is trembling like a fiery veil between
The blue sky and the Earth ; and the far stars
Glimmer but faintly through it.   Day hath left
No traces of its presence, and the blush
With which it welcomed the embrace of Night
Has faded from the sky's blue cheek, as fades
The blush of human beauty, when the tone
Or look which woke its evidence of love,
Hath passed away forever.   Wherefore then
Burns the strange fire in Heaven ?—It is as if
Nature's last curse—the terrible plague of fire,
Were working in her elements, and the sky
Consuming like a vapor.

Lo—a change !
The fiery flashes sink, and all along
The dim horizon of the fearful North,
Rests a broad crimson, like a sea of blood,
Untroubled by a wave.   And lo—above,
Bendeth a luminous arch of pale, pure white,
Clearly contrasted with the blue above
And the dark red beneath it.   Glorious !
How like a pathway for the sainted ones—
The pure and beautiful intelligences,
Who minister in Heaven, and offer up
Their praise as incense ; or, like that which rose
Before the pilgrim-prophet, when the tread
Of the most holy angels brightened it,
And in his dream the haunted sleeper saw
The ascending and descending of the blest !

Another change.   Strange, fiery forms uprise
On the wide arch, and take the throngful shape
Of warriors gathering to the strife on high,—
A dreadful marching of infernal shapes,
Beings of fire with plumes of bloody red,
With banners flapping o'er their crowded ranks,
And long swords quivering up against the sky !
And now they meet and mingle ; and the ear
Listens with painful earnestness to catch

The ring of cloven helmets and the groan
Of the down-trodden.   But there comes no sound,
Save a low, sullen rush upon the air,
Such as the unseen wings of spirits make,
Sweeping the void above us.   All is still.
Yet falls each red sword fiercely, and the hoof
Of the wild steed is crushing on the breast
Of the o'erthrown and vanquished.   'Tis a strange
And awful conflict—an unearthly war !
It is as if the dead had risen up
To battle with each other—the stern strife
Of spirits visible to mortal eyes.

Steed, plume and warrior vanish one by one,
Wavering and changing to unshapely flame :
And now across the red and fearful sky,
A long, bright flame is trembling, like the sword
Of the great Angel at the guarded gate
Of Paradise, when all the sacred groves
And beautiful flowers of Eden-land blushed red
Beneath its awful shadow ; and the eye
Of the lone outcasts quailed before its glare,
As from the immediate questioning of God.

And men are gazing on that troubled sky
With most unwonted earnestness, and fair

And beautiful brows are reddening in the light
Of that strange vision of the upper air ;
Even as the dwellers of Jerusalem,
The leagured of the Roman, when the sky
Of Palestine was thronged with fiery shapes,
And from Antonia's tower, the mailed Jew
Saw his own image pictured in the air,
Contending with the heathen ; and the priest,
Beside the Temple's altar, veiled his face
From that most horrid phantasy, and held
The censor of his worship, with a hand
Shaken by terror's palsy.

        It has passed—
And Heaven again is quiet ; and its stars
Smile down serenely.   There is not a stain
Upon its dream-like loveliness of blue—
No token of the fiery mystery
Which made the evening fearful.   But the hearts.
Of those who gazed upon it, yet retain
The shadow of its awe—the chilling fear
Of its ill-boding aspect.   It is deemed
A revelation of the things to come—
Of war and its calamities—the storm
Of the pitched battle, and the midnight strife
Of heathen inroad—the devouring flame,

The dripping tomahawk, the naked knife,
The swart hand twining with the silken locks
Of the fair girl—the torture, and the bonds
Of perilous captivity with those
Who know not mercy, and with whom revenge
Is sweeter than the cherished gift of life.

THE LAST NORRIDGEWOCK.

The Norridgewocks--a bold and vigorous race of the New-England Red
men, perished in their struggle with the English. Taconet, the last Sachem,
fell in battle, soon after the death of Ralle, the French Jesuit, whose adventures in the New World are full of romance. It is said that the last survivor of the tribe was a female descendant of this Chief.]

SHE stood beneath the shadow of an oak,
Grim with uncounted winters, and whose boughs
Had sheltered in their youth the giant forms
Of the great Chieftain's warriors. She was fair,
Even to a white man's vision--and she wore
A blended grace and dignity of mein
Which might befit the daughter of a King--
The queenliness of nature. She had all
The magic of proportion which might haunt
The dream of some rare painter, or steal in
Upon the musings of the statuary,
Like an unreal vision. She was dark,--
There was no play of crimson on her cheek,
Yet were her features beautiful. Her eye
Was clear and wild—and brilliant as a beam
Of the live sunshine ; and her long, dark hair
Sway'd in rich masses to th' unquiet wind.

The West was glad with sunset.--Over all
The green hills and the wilderness there fell
A great and sudden glory.   Half the sky
Was full of glorious tints, as if the home
And fountain of the rainbow were revealed ;
And through its depth of beauty looked the star
Of the blest Evening, like an Angel's eye.

The Indian watched the sunset—and her eye
Glistened one moment—then a tear fell down—
For she was dreaming of her fallen race—
The mighty who had perished—for her creed
Had taught her that the spirits of the brave
And beautiful were gathered in the West—
The Red man's Paradise;--and then she sang
Faintly her song of sorrow, with a low
And half-hushed tone, as if she knew that those
Who listened were unearthly auditors,
And that the dead had bowed themselves to hear.

" The moons of Autumn wax and wane--the sound of
    swelling floods
Is borne upon the mournful wind ; and broadly on the
    woods
The colours of the changing leaves—the fair, frail
    flowers of frost,

Before the round and yellow sun most beautiful are
    tossed.

The morning breaketh with a clear, bright pencilling
    of sky,

And blushes through its golden clouds, as the great
    Sun goes by ;

And Evening lingers in the West—more beautiful
    than dreams

Which whisper of the Spirit-land, its wilderness and
    streams !

A little time—another moon—the forest will be
    sad—

The streams will mourn the pleasant light which made
    their journey glad ;

The morn will faintly lighten up—the sunlight glisten
    cold,

And wane into the western sky without its Autumn
    gold.

And yet I weep not for the sign of desolation near—

The ruin of my hunter-race may only ask a tear,—

The wailing streams will laugh again—the naked trees
    put on

The beauty of their summer green beneath the sum-
    mer sun—

The Autumn-cloud will yet again its crimson draperies
    fold—

The star of sunset smile again—a diamond set in
    gold!

But never, for their forest-lake—or for their mountain-
    path,

The mighty of our race shall leave the hunting-ground
    of Death.

I know the tale my fathers told—the legend of their
    fame—

The glory of our spotless race before the pale ones
    came—

When, asking fellowship of none—by turns the foe
    of all—

The death-bolts of our vengeance fell, as Heaven's
    own lightnings fall ;

When, at the call of Taconet, my warrior-sire of old,

The war-shout of a thousand men upon the midnight
    rolled ;

And fearless and companionless our warriors strode
    alone,

And from the big lake to the sea the green earth was
    their own.

Where are they now ? Around their changed and
    stranger-peopled home,

Full sadly o'er their thousand graves the flowers of
    Autumn bloom—

The bow of strength is buried with the calamut and
　　spear,
And the spent arrow slumbereth, forgetful of the
　　deer !
The last canoe is rotting by the lake it glided o'er,
When dark-eyed maidens sweetly sang its welcome
　　from the shore.
The foot-prints of the hunter-race from all the hills
　　have gone—
Their offerings to the Spirit-land have left the altar-
　　stone—
The ashes of the council-fire have no abiding token—
The song of war has died away—the Powwah's charm
　　is broken—
The startling war-whoop cometh not upon the loud,
　　clear air,—
The ancient woods are vanishing—the pale men
　　gather there.

And who is left to mourn for this?—a solitary one,
Whose life is waning into death like yonder setting
　　sun !—
A broken reed—a faded flower, that lingereth behind,
To mourn above its fallen race, and wrestle with the
　　wind !
Lo—from the Spirit-land I hear the voices of the blest ;
The holy faces of the loved are leaning from the
　　West.

The mighty and the beautiful—the peerless ones of
        old—

They call me to their pleasant sky and to their thrones
        of gold ;—

Ere the spoilers' eye hath found me, when there are
        none to save—

Or the evil-hearted pale-face made the free of soul a
        slave—

Ere the step of air grow weary, or the sunny eye be
        dim,

The Father of my people is calling me to him."